Gleanings from Pittsburgh & W. Pa.: Newspaper &c, Views, 1786-1886

By
J. K. Folmar I

Yohogania Press
California, Pennsylvania
2006

Published by:

YOHOGANIA PRESS
P. O. Box 692
California, Pa. 15419

Other Yohogania Books by the author:

*Drifting Back in Time: Historical Sketches of
Washington and Fayette Counties, Pennsylvania,
including the Monongahela River Valley, 2005.*

*Monongahela City Anniversary 1792-1892,
Originally Published 1895, Reprinted 2004,
with Introduction and Index.*

ISBN: 978-0-9630513-4-9
LCCN: 2006938525
Printed in the U.S.A.

Dedicated to
my beloved sister
Jacqueline ("Jackie")
Elizabeth Folmar Presley
and her husband
(Robert) Jerry Presley (1941-2004).

Contents

Illustrations

Introduction

My interest in local history began when I walked into an old schoolhouse in Greensboro, Pa., while on a Sunday afternoon drive in 1979. A group was organizing the Monongahela River Buffs Association. I joined and when the editor of its newsletter suddenly died, I agreed to take on the job, temporarily. I have edited *The Voice of the Mon* since. I, of course, had to find data for it. I began to research the history of the river, and gradually, developed an interest in the history of the region. I soon included local history in my courses in early U. S. History at California University of Pennsylvania. Also, a course in Local History became one of my offerings. Local nineteenth century newspapers (the University has an excellent collection) became a primary source of information for my courses and for the newsletter.

This project began years ago. Other research delayed its completion. My initial plan was to edit articles from local newspapers which described local sites in the early 1800s. In time, I decided to move the date to the 1870s. Recently, I extended the timeline to 1886. Methodologically, there were fewer items to choose from in the early years; they increased in numbers and length as newspaper technology improved with the transition from weeklies to dailies.

Why develop this project? Initially, I had been unable to find any publications that use local descriptions, in its entirety, from local papers. Hence, this is a first! Too, these commentaries are, often — except from letters — the only sources available which reflect the local "culture," including how people travelled, thought, lived, played, and survived for over a century. Geographical comments are abundant — from Pittsburgh to local communities and rural areas. The earlier descriptions are "historically" oriented. Also, the comments range from purely descriptive comments in the early years to extravagant excursions in the 1870s. Also, these descriptions reflect how writers, from elites and newspapermen to locals signing their pieces with initials or a single letter, viewed the world in which they lived — unaware that they would be read over a century later. Their commentaries range from laudatory "boosterism" to critical observations. Names, industries (small and large), means of transport, flood information, fairs, social life and celebrations are parts of this century of local life. It should, also, provide a new source for genealogists and students of local history.

Thirty of the forty-four articles, or sixty-eight per cent are from the *Pittsburgh Gazette,* which include five articles from other newspapers and one from a directory. Six articles are from the *Pittsburgh Post,* two from the *Monongahela Republican,* and one each from the *Brownsville American Telegraph* and *Harris' Intelligencer.* There are four non-newspaper pieces: three from Z. Cramer's *Navigator* and one from S. Jones' *Pittsburgh Sketches.*

Ten articles relate to Pittsburgh directly, and the eight on floods include the city, of course, as do the three from Cramer's *Navigator.* (The latter also has data on Virginia locations.) Three describe the coming of the railroads, and two each are about Washington, Pa., the Cheat River, and "tours" of Fayette County. In addition, there are pieces on towns, villages, rural sites, as well as tours on the rivers and railroads. The only lengthy non-Pennsylvania article is the excursion by University of Pittsburgh elites to Chautaugua, N. Y. Although there is an emphasis on Pittsburgh — from village to "smoky city" — the last fourteen articles, from 1861 to 1886, are about other sites, except for the three floods.

I am most appreciative to Mary Beth Graf for typing the original manuscript, formatting the illustrations, and compiling the index, and to William Reed for the cover design. I am also grateful to two staff members in Manderino Library at California University for their many "aids" when using the microfilm readers and locating sources: Dan Zyglowicz, Government Documents and Virginia Sharrer, Serials Section.

Dr. J. K. Folmar I
California, Pa.
December 2006

1

The Pittsburgh Gazette was the first newspaper west of the Alleghenies. John Scull and Joseph Hall founded it in the summer of 1786. This article was written by Hugh H. Brackenridge. Born in Scotland, he was brought to Pennsylvania at age 5. He attended Princeton and came "west" in 1781. He became a prominent "pioneer" leader in Pittsburgh's early history and was chiefly responsible for the chartering the Pittsburgh Academy, the incorporation of the Presbyterian Congregation, and, as a legislator, the erection of Allegheny County in 1788. He is credited with coaxing the two printers to come to Pittsburgh and would write many articles in the paper. His aim in this article is to attract migrants to the region. I could not find a copy of the original; this is an 1858 reprint.

* * * * * * *

Pittsburgh Daily Gazette, November 23, 1858
"PITTSBURGH IN 1786.

As the approaching Centennial [of the fall of Ft. Duquesne to the British in 1758 during the 'French and Indian War'] has set every one upon hunting up reminiscences, we present to our readers, the first newspaper account of this city that was ever published. It is from –
The Pittsburgh *Gazette* of July 20, 1786.

The Allegheny river running from the north-east, and the Monongahela from the south-west, meet at the angle of about thirty-three degrees, and form the Ohio. This is said to signify, in some of the Indian languages, bloody; so that the Ohio river may be translated the River of Blood. The French have called it La Belle Riviere, that is, the Beautiful or Fair River, but this is not intended by them as having any relation to the name Ohio.

It may have received the name of Ohio about the beginning of the present century, when the Six Nations [Iroquois] made war upon their fellow savages in these territories, and subjected several tribes.

The word Monongahela is said to signify, in some of the Indian languages, the Falling-in-Banks, that is, the stream of the Falling-in, or Mouldering Banks.

At a distance of about four or five hundred yards from the head of the Ohio, is a small island, lying to the northwest side of the river, at the distance of seventy yards from the shore. It is covered with wood, and at the lowest part is a lofty hill, famous for the number of wild turkeys which inhabit it. The island is not more in length than one quarter of a mile, and in breadth about one hundred yards. A small space on the upper end is cleared and overgrown with grass. The savages had cleared it during the late war, a party of them attached to the United States having placed their wigwams and raised corn there. The Ohio, at the distance of about one mile from its sources, winds round the lower end of the island, and disappears. I call the confluence of the Allegheny and the Monongahela the source of the Ohio.

It is pleasant to observe the conflict of these two waters where they meet: when of an equal height the contest is equal, and a small rippling appears from the point of land at their junction to the distance of about five hundred yards. When the Allegheny is master, as the term is, the current keeps its course a great way into the Monongahela, before it is overcome and falls into the bed of the Ohio. The Monongahela, in like manner having mastery, bears away the Allegheny, and with its muddy waters discolors the crystal current of that river. This happens frequently inasmuch as these two rivers, coming from different climates of the country, are seldom swollen at the same time. The flood of the Allegheny rises perhaps the highest. I have observed it to have been at least thirty feet above the level, by the impression of the ice on the branches of trees which overhang the river, and had been cut at the breaking up of the winter, when the snow and frost, melting toward the north-east, throw themselves down with amazing rapidity and violence in a mighty deluge. The current of the Allegheny is in general more rapid than that of the Monongahela, and though not broader or of greater depth, yet, from this circumstance throws forward a greater quantity of water in the same space of time. In this river, at the distance of about a mile above the town of Pittsburgh, is a beautiful little [Herrs] island, which, if there are river gods and nymphs, they may be supposed to haunt. At the upper end of the island, and toward the western shore, is a small ripple, as it is called, where the water, bubbling as if it sprung from the pebbles of the fountain, gives vivacity and an air of cheerfulness to the scene.

The fish of the Allegheny are harder and firmer than those of the Monongahela or Ohio, owing, as is supposed, to the greater coldness and purity of the water. The fish in general of those rivers are good. They are the pike, weighing frequently fifteen or twenty pounds; the perch, much larger than any I have ever seen in the bay of Chesapeake, which is the only tide from whence I have ever seen perch; there is also sturgeon, and many other kinds of fish.

It is high amusement to those who are fond of fishing, to angle in those waters, more especially at the time of a general flood, when the frequent nibbles of the large and small fishes entertain the expectations, and sometimes gratify it by a bite, and when those of the larger size are taken, it is necessary to play them a considerable time before it can be judged safe to draw them in. I have seen a canoe half loaded in a morning by some of those most expert in the employment, but you will see in a spring evening the banks of the river lined with men fishing, at intervals from one another.

This, with the streams gently gliding, the woods, at a distance, green, and the shadows lengthening toward the town, forms a delightful scene. Fond of the water, I have been sometimes highly pleased in going with a select party, in a small barge, up or down the rivers, and landing at a cool spring, to enjoy the verdant turf, amidst the shady bowers of ash-wood, sugar-tree, or oak, planted by the hand of nature, not art.

It may be said by some who will read this description which I have given, or may be about to give, that it is minute and useless, inasmuch as they are observations of things well known. But let it be considered, that it is not intended for the people of this country, but for those at a distance, who may not yet be acquainted with the natural situation of the town of Pittsburgh, or having heard of it, may wish to be more particularly informed. Who knows that families of fortune it may induce to emigrate to this place?

There is a rock known by the name of M'Kee's rock, at the distance of about three miles below the head of the Ohio. It is the end of a promontory, where the river bends to the north west, and where, by the rushing of the floods, the earth has been cut away during several ages, so that now the huge overhanging rocks appear, hollowed beneath, so as to make a dome of majesty and grandeur, near one hundred feet in heighth. Here are the names of French and British officers engraved, who in former times, in parties of pleasure, had visited this place. The town of Pittsburgh, at the head of the Ohio, is scarcely visible from hence, by means of an intervening [Brunot] island, the lower end of which is nearly opposite the rocks. Just below them, at the bending of the river, is a deep eddy water, which has been wounded by a line of thirty fathoms, and no bottom found. Above them is a beautiful extend of bottom, containing five or six hundred acres, and the ground rising to the inland country with an easy ascent, so as to form an extensive landscape. As you ascend the river from these rocks, to the town of Pittsburgh, you pass by on your right hand the mouth of a brook known by the name of Saw-mill run. This empties itself about half a mile below the town, and is overlooked by a building on its banks, on the point of a hill which fronts the east, as is first struck by the beams of the rising sun. At a small distance from its mouth is a saw-mill, about twenty perches [330 feet] below the situation of an old mill built by the British, the remains of some parts of which are yet seen.

At the head of the Ohio stands the town of Pittsburgh, on an angular piece of ground, the two rivers forming the two sides of the angle. Just at the point stood, where I first came to this country, a tree, leaning against which I have often overlooked the wave, or committing my garments to its shade, have bathed in the transparent tide. How have I regretted its undeserved fate, when the early winter flood tore it from the roots, and left the bank bare.

On this point stood the old French Fort known by the name of Fort Du Quesne, which was evacuated and blown up by the French in the campaign of the British under Gen. [John] Forbes [on Nov. 24, 1758 during the 'French and Indian War.']. The appearance of the ditch and mound, with the salient angles and bastions still remains, so as to prevent that perfect level of the ground which otherwise would exist. It has been long overgrown with the finest verdure and depastured on by cattle; but since the town has been laid out it has been enclosed, and buildings are erected.

Just above these works is the present garrison [of Ft. Pitt] built by Gen [John] Stanwix [in 1859-60], and is said to have cost the crown of Britain $60,000. Be that as it may, it has been a work of great labor and of little use – for, situated on a plain, it is commanded by heights and rising grounds in every side, and some at less than the distance of a mile. The fortification is regular, constructed according to the rules of art, and about three years ago put into good repair by Gen. [William] Irwin[e], who commanded at this post. It has the advantage of an excellent magazine, built of stone; but the time is come, and it hoped will not again return, when the use of this garrison is at an end. There is a line of [military] posts below it on the Ohio river, to the distance of three hundred miles. The savages come to this place for trade, not for war, and any future contact that we may have with them, will be on the heads of the more northern rivers that fall into the Mississippi.

The bank of the Allegheny river, on the north-west side of the town of Pittsburgh, is planted with an orchard of apple trees, with some pear trees intermixed. These were brought, it is said, and planted by a British officer, who commanded at this place early on the first occupation of it by the crown of England. He has deserved the thanks of those who have since enjoyed it, as the fruit is excellent, and the trees bear in abundance every year. Near the garrison on the Allegheny bank, were formerly what were called the king's artillery gardens, delightful spots, cultivated highly to usefulness and pleasure, the soil favoring the growth of plants and flowers, equal with any on the globe. Over this ground the ancient herbs and plants springing up underneath the foot, it is delightful still to walk, covered with the orchard shade.

On the margin of this river once stood a row of houses, elegant and neat, and not unworthy of the European taste, but they have been swept away in the course of time, some for forming an opening to the river from the garrison, that the artillery might incommode the enemy approaching and deprived of shelter; some torn away by the fury of the rising river, indignant of too near a pressure on its banks. These buildings were the receptacles of the ancient Indian trade, which, coming from the westward, centered in this quarter;

but of these buildings, like decayed monuments of grandeur, no trace remains. Those, who twenty years ago, saw them flourish, can only say, here they stood.

From the verdant walk on the margin of this beautiful river, you have a view of an island about a mile above, round which the river twines with a re-splendent brightness; gliding on the eastern bank, it would wish to keep a straight direction, once supposed to be its course; but thrown beneath, it modestly sub-mits, and falls toward the town. When the poet comes with his enchanting song to pour his magic numbers on this scene, this little island may aspire to live with those in the Aegean sea, where the song of Homer drew the image of delight, or where the [English river] Cam or [Egyptian goddess of fertility] Isis, embracing in their bosoms gems like these, are sung by [John] Milton, father of the modern bards.

(To Be Concluded Tomorrow)

* * * * * * *

Pittsburgh Daily Gazette, November 25, 1858
" . . . *The Pittsburgh Gazette* of July 29, 1786
(Concluded)

On the west side of the Allegheny river, and opposite the orchard, is a level of three thousand acres, reserved by the State to be laid out in lots for the purpose of a town. A small stream, at right angles to the river, passes through it. On this ground it is supposed a town may stand; but on all hands it is excluded from the praise of being a situation so convenient as on the side of the river where the present town is placed; yet it is a most delightful grove of oak, cherry and walnut trees; but we return and take a view of the Mononga-hela, on the southern side of the town.

This bank is closely set with buildings, for the distance of near half a mile, and behind this range the town chiefly lies, falling back on the plains between the two rivers. To the eastward is Grant's hill, a beautiful rising ground, discovering marks of ancient cultivation; the forests having long ago withdrawn, and shown the head and brow beset with green and flowers. From this hill two crystal fountains issue, which in the heat of summer continue with a limpid current to refresh the taste. It is pleasant to celebrate a festival on the summit of this ground. In the year 1781, a bower had been erected, covered with green shrubs. The sons and daughters of the day assembling, joined in the festivity, viewing the rivers at a distance, and listening to the music of the military on the plain beneath them. When the moonlight rising from the east had softened into gray, the prospect, a lofty pile of wood enflamed, with pyramidical rising, illuminated both the rivers and the town, which far around reflected brightness. Approaching in the appearance of a river god, a swain begirt with weeds natural to those streams, and crowned with leaves of the sugar tree, hailed us, and gave prophetic hints of the grandeur of our future empire. His words I remember not, but it seemed to me for a moment, that the mystic agencies of deities well known in Greece and Rome, was not a fable; but that powers unseen haunt the woods and rivers, who take part in the affairs of mortals, and are pleased with the celebration of events that spring from great achievements, and from virtue.

This is the hill, and from whence it takes its name, where in the ['French and Indian'] war which terminated in the year 1763, [Major James] Grant advancing with about eight hundred Caledonians or Highland Scotch troops, beat a reveille a little after sunrise to the French garrison, who, accompanied with a number of savages, sallied out and flanking him unseen from the bottom on the left and right, then covered with wood, ascended the hill, tomahawked and cut his troops to pieces, and made Grant himself a prisoner.[1] Bones and weapons are yet found on the hill – the bones white with the weather, the weapons covered with rust.

On the summit of the hill is a mound of earth, supposed to be a catacomb or ancient burying place of the savages. There can be no doubt of this, as on the opening some of the like tumuli, or hills of earth, bones are found. In places where stones are plenty, these mounds are raised of stones, and skeletons are found in them. To the north-east of Grant's hill, there is one still higher, at the distance of about a quarter of a mile, which is called the Quarry hill, from the excellent stone quarry that has been opened in it. From this hill there is an easy descent the whole way to the town, and an excellent smooth road, so that the stones can be easily procured to erect any building at Pittsburgh. From the Quarry hill you have a view of four or five miles of the Allegheny river, along which lies a fine bottom, and in high cultivation, with different inclosures and farmhouses, the river winding through the whole prospect.

This hill would seem to stand as that whereon a strong redoubt might be placed, to command the commerce of the Allegheny river, while directly opposite, on the Monongahela side, to the south-east, stands a hill of the same height and appearance, known by the name of Ayres' hill, so called from a British engineer of that name, who gave his opinion in favor of this ground as that whereon the fort ought to be constructed, as being the highest ground, and which must command the rivers, and the plain with the inferior rising grounds on which the town is built. The hill has been culti-

---

[1]Grant and eighteen prisoners were taken to Canada. The first British governor of east Florida, 1763-1771, he was a major general during the American Revolution.

PITTSBURGH IN 1790. From a steel engraving by J. C. McRae.
Source: George T. Fleming, *Fleming's View of Old Pittsburgh.*
A Portfolio of the Past., ed. Henry Russell Miller
(Pittsburgh: The Crescent Press, 1932).

vated on the summit by a Highland regiment, who built upon it, though the buildings are now gone, and the brow of the hill is still covered with wood.

From the Ayres hill issue several fountains, falling chiefly toward the north, into a small brook, which increasing, encircles the foot of the hill, and takes its course through several beautiful little meads into the Monongahela river. On this brook, before it takes it turn to the Monongahela, is a delightful little valley, and in the neighborhood of some plum trees, the natives of the country, was the ancient residence of a certain Anthony Thompson, the vestiges of whose habitation still remain; an extent of ground cleared by him lies to the north, accustomed to long cultivation, and now thrown out a common. The best brick may be made from this ground, the fine loam and sand of which the soil consists, and the water just at hand, highly favoring the object.

As you ascend from the valley, through which a main leading road passes from the country, you see Monongahela, and approaching Grant's hill on the right, you have the point of view from whence the town is seen to the best advantage.[2] It is hid from you until by the winding of the road you begin to turn the point of the hill; you then see house by house on the Monongahela side opening to your view, until you are in front of the main town, in a direct line to the confluence of the rivers. Then the buildings on the Allegheny show themselves, with the plain extending to the right, which had been concealed. You have in the meantime a view of the rising grounds beyond the rivers, crowned with lofty woods. I was once greatly struck on a summer morning, viewing from the ground the early vapor rising from the river. It hung midway between the foot and summit of the hill, so that the green above had the appearance of an island.

It may be observed, that at the junction of these two rivers, until eight o'clock of summer mornings, a light fog is usually incumbent, but it is of a salutary nature, inasmuch as it consists of vapor not exhaled from stagnant water, but which the sun of the preceding day had extracted from trees and flowers, and in the evening had sent back in dew, so that rising with a second sun in fog, and becoming of aromatic quality, it is experienced to be healthful.

The town of Pittsburgh, as at present built, stands chiefly on what is called the third bank; that is the third rising of the ground above the Allegheny water. For there is the first bank, which confines the river at the present time; and about three hundred feet removed is a second, like the falling of a garden; then a third, at the distance of about three hundred yards; and lastly, a fourth bank, all easy of inclination

---

[2]In order for Pittsburgh to expand, Grant's Hill, soon known as "the Hump," had to be lowered. The first effort began in 1836. Additional cuts were made in 1844 and 1847. The final cut was in 1911/12. The total reduction, in some places, was over sixty feet.

and parallel with the Allegheny river. These banks would seem in successive periods to have been the margin of the river, which gradually has changed its course, and has been thrown from one descent to another, to the present bed where it lies. In digging wells the kinds of stones are found which we observe in the Allegheny current, worn smooth by the attrition of the water. Shells also intermixed with these are thrown out. Nature, therefore, or the river, seems to have formed the bed of this town as a garden with level walks, and fallings of the ground. Hence the advantage of descending gardens on these banks, which art elsewhere endeavors, with the greatest industry, to form. Nor is the soil less happy than the situation. The mold is light and rich. The finest gardens in the known world may be formed here.

The town consists at present of about an hundred dwelling houses, with buildings appurtenant. More are daily added, and for some time past it has improved with an equal but continued pace. The inhabitants, children, men and women, are about fifteen hundred; this number;* doubling almost every year, from the accession of people from abroad, and from those born in the town. As I pass along, I may remark that this new country is in general highly prolific; whether it is that the vegotable air, if I may so express it, constantly perfumed with aromatic flavor, and impregnated with salts drawn from the fresh soil, is more favorable to the production of men and other animals than decayed grounds.

There is not a more delightful spot under heaven to spend any of the summer months than at this place. I am astonished that there should be such repairing to the Warm Springs in Virginia, a place pent up between two hills, where the sun pours its beams concentrated as in a burning-glass, and not a breath of air stirs; where the eye can wander scarcely half a furlong, while here we have the breezes of the river, coming from the Mississippi and the ocean; the gales that fan the woods, and are sent from the refreshing lakes to the northward; in the meantime the prospect of extensive hills and dales, whence the fragrant air brings odors of a thousand flowers and plants, or of the corn and grain of husbandmen, upon its balmy wings. Here we have the town and country together. How pleasant it is in a summer evening, to walk out upon these grounds, the smooth green surface of the earth, and the woodland shade softening the late fervid beams of the sun; how pleasant by a crystal fountain is a tea party under one of these hills, with the rivers and the plains beneath.

Nor is the winter season enjoyed with less festivity than in more populous and cultivated towns. The buildings warm; fuel abundant, consisting of the finest coal from the neighboring hills, or of ash, hickory, or oak, brought down in rafts by the rivers. In the meantime, the climate is less severe at this place than on the other side of the mountain, lying deep in the bosom of the wood; sheltered on the northeast by the bending of the Allegheny heights, and the southwest warmed by the tepid winds from the bay of Mexico and the great southern ocean.

In the fall of the year, and during the winter season, there is usually a great concourse of strangers at this place, from the different States, about to descend the river to the westward, or to make excursions into the uninhabited and adjoining country. These, with the inhabitants of the town, spend the evening in parties at the different houses, or at public balls, where they are surprised to find an elegant assembly of ladies, not to be surpassed in beauty and accomplishments perhaps by any on the continent.

It must appear like enchantment to a stranger, who after traveling an hundred miles from the settlements, across a dreary mountain, and through the adjoining country, where in many places the spurs of the mountain still continue, and cultivation does not always show itself, to see, all at once, and almost on the verge of the inhabited globe, a town with smoking chimneys, halls lighted up with splendor, ladies and gentlemen assembled, various music, and the mazes of the dance. He may suppose it to be the effect of magic, or that he is come into a new world where there is all the refinement of the former, and more benevolence of heart.

*This estimate of the population is a most extravagant one, being about fifteen to a house, which is incredible.-[Major Isaac] Craig."[3]

Note: In 1788, Allegheny County was carved out of Westmoreland and Washington Counties. It was huge and, in 1792, the Erie Triangle was purchased by the state and tacked on. In 1800, the county was reduced to its present size with the creation of eight new counties and parts of two. In 1794, Pittsburgh was incorporated as a borough.

❧

---

[3]Irish-born, Craig came to Philadelphia in 1765/66 where he became a master carpenter. He served during the Revolution, first at sea as a marine, then as an artillery officer. He was at Ft. Pitt from 1781-83. With war's end, he was a co-purchaser of land from the Penn family on which Pittsburgh would emerge. In 1787, he was appointed deputy quartermaster and military storekeeper. He managed all of the military preparations for the next thirteen years, including supplying the troops in the "Indian wars," and building (and naming) Ft. Fayette .25 miles up the Allegheny River.

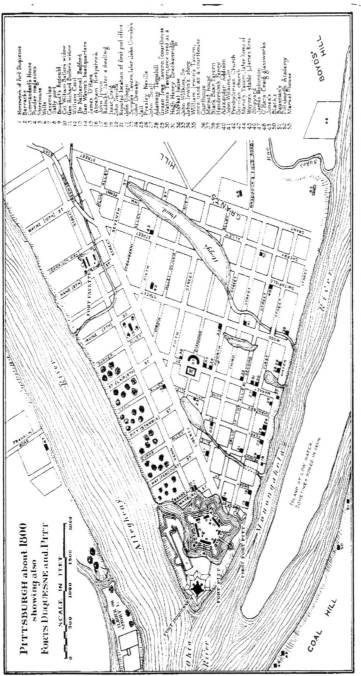

Source: George E. Kelly, ed., *Allegheny County: A Sesqui-Centennial Review 1788-1938* (Pittsburgh: Allegheny County Sesqui-Centennial Committee, 1938).

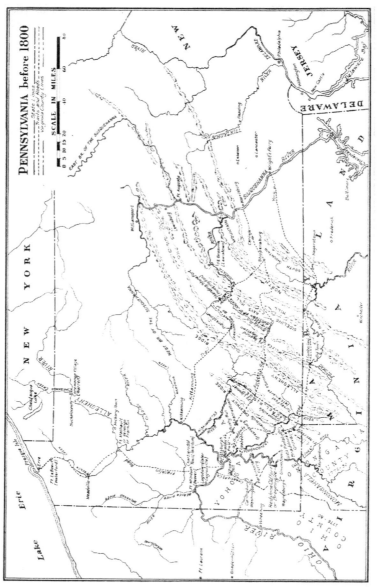

Source: Kelly, *Allegheny County: A Sesqui-Centennial Review 1788-1938.*

2

THE NAVIGATOR, 1802

Zadok Cramer was born in New Jersey and grew up in Washington County. In 1800, at the age of 27, he set up a bookbinding and publishing shop in Pittsburgh. He soon had a circulating library, a bookstore and a paper mill. He published almanacs and other books but, by far, his most well-known publication was a guide for the rivers, soon known as the *Navigator.* Published from 1801 until 1824, it ran through twelve editions.

The earliest existing edition is the "Third Corrected Edition" of 1802, contained ca. 40 pages for twenty-five cents. The title, covering an entire page, is, in part: "The Ohio and Mississippi NAVIGATOR Comprising an Ample Account of Those Beautiful Rivers, From the Head of the Former, to the Mouth of the Latter. A particular description of the several TOWNS, POSTS, CAVES, PORTS, HAROURS &c. on their banks, and accurate directions. How to Navigate them, . . . and the Distances From Place to Place. Together with a description Of MONONGAHELA AND ALLEGHENY RIVERS."

His 1802 descriptions of the early "towns" were, initially, taken from "the Journals of Gentlemen of observation, and now minutely corrected by several persons who have navigated those rivers for fifteen and twenty years." As with Brackenridge, Cramer is a "booster" for the region, particularly --

"PITTSBURGH

No island town in the United States can boast of a superior situation to this, both as to its beauty, as also with respect to the many advantages with which it is attended: being delightfully situated at the head of the Ohio river, on the point of land formed by the junction of the Allegheny and

Monongahela rivers. The seite [sic] of the old French garrison Du Quesne, which was taken by general [John] Forbes in the year 1758, is immediately at the confluence of the two rivers and commands an elegant view of each, as well as of the Ohio. The British garrison, Fort Pitt, so called after the late [William Pitt] Earl of Chatham, and erected adjacent to the former, higher up on the Monongahela, was formerly a place of some consequence to the annals of frontier settlements, but fell into decay on its being given up by its founders.

Being included in one of the manors of the Penn family, it was sold by the proprietors, and now makes a part of the town of Pittsburgh, and is laid out in town lots. Fort Fayette, built a very few years since [in 1792], is also within the limits of the town, on the bank of the Allegheny . . . a garrison is at present kept here, and for the most part, is made head quarters for the United States army.

The local situation of the town is so very commanding, that it has been emphatically called the key to the Western Country, its natural one is particularly handsome. Blessed as it is with numerous advantages, there is nothing surprising in its having encrased rapidly within a few years past.—It contains near 400 dwelling houses, many of them large and elegantly built with brick; and about 2,000 inhabitants. It abounds with mechanics that carry on most of the different manufactures that are to be met with in any other part of the United States, -- and contains near 40 retail stores, all of which seem continually busy. It is here where most of the goods waggoned over the mountains in spring and fall, and destined for the Kentuckey and New Orleans trade, are brought to be ready for embarkation [by flatboats and keelboats.]

Many valuable Manufactories have been established in this place very lately; among which are, those of glass, nails, tobacco, &c. – The manufacture of glass is carried on extensively, and of an excellent quality: Two glass works have been erected, the one for the courser kind of glass has been doing business for some time; the other for the finer glass is about to be put in motion.   This manufactory may be reckoned among the fist that is of the utmost importance to this country; and must consequently prove an immense saving to it. – It richly merits all that consideration justly due from an enlightened people.

Shipbuilding in and near this place deserves notice – several are now on the stocks at this place, and one a small distance up the Allegheny river was lately launched, of 160 tons burden.[1] I think we may say, without being presumed to boast, that there is no place in the United States, whose inhabitants enjoy better health than those of Pittsburgh; notwithstanding our frequent changes of weather. – Having this invaluable blessing, with many other peculiar advantages, nothing ought to prevent them becoming an opulent and happy people."

Note: Pittsburgh's population in 1800? 1,565.

---

[1]Boatbuilding was a major industry in the region. The average flatboat, resembling floating boxes, was about 15 by 50 feet and carried 40-50 tons.   The "Kentucky" boats were partially roofed (about two-thirds) for protection from the weather for families and/ or storage of freight.   The sturdier "New Orleans" boats were roofed over the entire length for the 2000+ mile trip to New Orleans.   Controlled by large sweeps or oars on the sides and one sweep in the stern which acted as a rudder, they provided the cheapest one-way transportation downriver for decades.   Keelboats were built on a keel, were long (50-80 feet) and narrow (6-12') with a 10-30 ton capacity.   They could be poled upstream and dominated two-way river travel until the coming of the steamboats in the 1820s.   There was also shipbuilding, primarily between 1801-1808. These rather small ships could be built cheaply, avoided the costs of transshipment from flatboats in New Orleans, and could sail directly to foreign markets.

A "Kentucky" flatboat (foreground) and keelboats in the background,
one being poled and one using its sail.
Source: *The Keelboat Age on Western Waters*, by Leland D. Baldwin (1969)
Reprinted by permission of the University of Pittsburgh Press.

Up the Monongahela River, there were only seven "towns" mentioned by Cramer in 1802, beginning with:

"MORGANTOWN . . .

is a flourishing [Virginia] town, pleasantly situated on the E. side of the Monongahela river, contains about 60 dwellings, is a county town for the counties of Harrison, Monongalia, Ohio, and Randolph – it may be considered as the head of the Monongahela navigation. [102 miles upriver from Pittsburgh.]

Just below the mouth of Georges Creek, [20 miles downriver per Cramer – actually 17 @ Mile 85] is situated New Geneva, a thriving town, a place of much business, and is rendered famous by an extensive Glass Works in its vicinity, which make and export large quantities of excellent glass. Kentuckey [flatboats] and other boats are built here. A little below, and on the opposite side of the river, lies Greensburgh [Greensboro], a small village.

FREDERICKTOWN [is]

A small town pleasantly situated. [24 miles downriver per Cramer; actually 21 @ Mile 64.]

BRIDGEPORT

[7 miles downriver per Cramer, actually 8 @ Mile 56.]

A small thriving town, in a pleasant situation; and below the mouth of this [Dunlap's] creek lies.

BROWNSVILLE, (or Redstone)

This place is well known to migraters down the rivers. It is handsomely situated, but somewhat divided, a part lying on the first bank, and the greater part on the elevated second bank. It is a place of much business, and contains 90 houses and 500 souls. The settlement around it is excellent having some of the best merchant mills that we can boast of, and an extensive paper mill on Redstone creek, and the only one on this side of the mountains, if we except Kentuckey. Kentuckey [flatboats] and other boats are built here, very largely. An extensive rope walk is also carried on, and other valuable manufactories.[2]

WILLIAMSPORT [Monongahela --
18 miles downriver per Cramer; actually 24 @ Mile 32.]

This town is well situated, is growing in business, having a fine settlement, and is on the direct [Glade] road

---

[2]Fayette County was established in 1783 and Brownsville was laid out by Thomas Brown in 1785 The former Nemacolin Trail (later Braddock's Road and currently Route 40) was a major transmontane "migraters" route from Cumberland, Md., to Brownsville on the Monongahela. They then proceeded downriver in flatboats. Brownsville was incorporated as a borough in 1815.

from Philadelphia to Washington, [Pa.], Wheelen [Wheeling], &c.

ELIZABETHTOWN [Elizabeth: 11 miles downriver
per Cramer; actually 9 at Mile 23.]

Is handsomely situated—much business is done here in the boat and ship way, The [brig] 'Monongahela Farmer' [in 1801] and other vessels of considerable burden were built here and loaded with the produce of the adjacent country, bound for the [Caribbean] Islands, &c.

M'KEESPORT [8 miles downriver at Mile 15.]

Is pleasantly situated below the junction of the Youghiogheny with the Monongahela. Many boats are built here, and, on this account, many migraters embark here destined for the lower country. -- This place is growing in business, and most probably will rise to considerable importance."

* * * * * * *

The locations up the "ALEGHENY [River]
Including the carrying place from the town of ERIE*

This town was, a few years since, laid out by direction of the legislature of the state of Pennsylvania – Taking into view its very important and commanding situation, they laid it out on a very large scale, and gave every encouragement to settlers in order to enhance its progress. For some time a prevailing fever deterred people from settling here. This obstacle has become nearly if not altogether removed. It now encreases rapidly, and commands an extensive trade through the lakes; and, in this respect, there is every probability of its becoming of the first importance to this country. A post office is established here, which receives the mail from Pittsburgh once every second week.

*Presqui'Isle [peninsula] — Owes its name to the peculiar manner in which the harbour is formed.

WATERFORD (LeBoeuf)

This town was also laid out by the state of Pennsylvania, and is encreasing. — Here was one of our western posts, which, but a few years since was evacuated. A post office is also kept here. [This was the portage route between French Creek and Erie –15 miles north. The French had a post here until 1763 and the U.S. until "peace" with the Indians in 1796.]

MEADVILLE
[ca. 86 miles north of Pittsburgh]

It is pleasantly situated on the bank of French Creek and is a thriving way, is a seat of justice for the counties of Erie, Mercer, Warren, Venango, and Crawford, in the latter of which it is situated. Here is also a post office – Considerable business is done, and contains about 50 houses and several stores.

FRANKLIN
[ca. 63 miles north of Pittsburgh.]

This town is situated immediately below the mouth of French creek, where it joins the Allegheny [River], is a post town, contains about 40 houses, several stores, and is a county town for Venango county.

FREEPORT

This town lies at the mouth of Buffaloe creek, which joins the Allegheny [River @ Mile 29] on the west and opposite to it comes in Kiskiminetas [River.]"

* * * * * * *

There are only two communities on the OHIO in Pennsylvania. Twenty-eight miles downriver is:

"M'INTOSH [present-day Beaver]

This town is handsomely situated on the N. west bank of the Ohio, about a quarter of a mile below the mouth of the

Big Beaver creek, [River]. Its situation is commanding, as there is at present a considerable, and in time must be a great trade up and down this creek the forces of which nearly reaching the borders of the Lake [Erie]. It is encreasing rapidly and contains several mercantile stores."

Ten miles [actually 12.5 @ Mile 39] farther down the river is:

"GEORGETOWN,

A small but flourishing town just above the mouth of Mill creek. It is pleasantly situated on a very high bank – A post office has been lately established there. Nearly opposite this place, a few yards from the other shore, a spring rises from the bottom of the river, which produces an oil similar to Seneca oil; which is thought to proceed from a large bed of mineral coal in the vicinity of the spring."

ﻌ

— 3 —

THE NAVIGATOR, 1806

This fifth edition added maps and illustrations and the "Account of [the] Louisiana [Purchase]." For

PITTSBURGH

his description contains much of the same information, as in 1802; however, there is more specificity. Fort Fayette now houses only "a small number of men," and the number of retail stores has increased from 40 to 50, and "The public buildings are, a court-house of brick, large and spacious, jail, market-house, four houses for public worship, the Episcopal church, the Presbyterian church, a church for the Covenanters, and one for the German Lutherans, these are all brick and handsomely built, the first is an octagon from and shews to great advantage; and an academy in which the languages are taught. The principal manufactories are, a glasshouse, an air-foundry, a cotton factory, three nail factories, three tin and copper factories, two factories of earthen ware, two rope-walks, a factory of hard and soft soap, a brush factory, two breweries, and four printing houses, three of which issue newspapers weekly, and the fourth prints books" Also, " . . . a new warehouse for the storage of merchandize has been recently erected on the Monongahela, Thomas Cromwall, proprietor." He lists the twelve ships, brigs, and schooners built for the West Indian and European trade, as well as a number of barges and keelboats. Kentucky and New Orleans flatboats were generally to be had ready made at the boat-yard of Sumrall, and M'collogh near the point.

"To strangers," he noted, "Pittsburgh has rather a gloomy appearance, arising from the smoke of the stone-coal of which about 170,000 bushels are consumed annually, these cost six cents per bushel, and are allowed to be the best in the world, they are remarkably sulpherous and make hot and lively fires. The inhabitants of this town having no places of public amusement, spend very little of their time in idleness; and although there are a superfluous number of taverns, intoxication is a vice but seldom to be seen stalking through the streets, gambling also is a species of wickedness very little practiced, and a general principle of honesty, industry, sobriety, and hospitality, prevails throughout the whole body of citizens.

Schools for teaching the mother tongue are numerous and tolerably well regulated; and there are also schools for drawing, dancing, sewing, embroidering, &c. schools for teaching the forte-piano, clarinet, flute, and violin.

A Bank of Discount and Deposit has been established in Pittsburgh within these last two years; it is a branch of the Pennsylvania Bank in Philadelphia; has sixteen directors, one of whom being the president, a cashier, a clerk, and a teller."

Up the MONONGAHELA,

Morgantown's description is the same, as in 1802; however, Cramer notes that it is "by water about 100 miles above Pittsburgh."

NEW GENEVA

is now "a small village." He mentions that the glass works was "erected by Albert Gallatin."

FREDERICK TOWN is a

"village [which] lies on the left side of the river on a high bank, is but small, contains two mercantile stores and a library instituted by Quakers, in Washington Co.

About one mile below this town, on the same side of the river, is a large and curious cave, called the 'Panthers' Den.' It enters the hill about half way up from its base. As you enter, the passage is low and descending; you have to slide down, or shove yourself half upright, for about fifteen yards with candles, and a cord as a director; here you enter a spacious room forty feet in diameter, not sufficiently high to stand upright in; wandering about for a while, you will discover to the left a fracture in the rock large enough to squeeze yourself through; here you creep up five feet into another considerable room, but so very low that you have either to crawl on your belly or roll over and over to make any progress; hunting about you will discover another small fracture to the right through which a middle sized man may force himself down a perpendicular of five feet, thence ten feet of a slope, and here you enter a room three times larger than either of the former; this room is divided by a petrified partition formed by the drippings of the roof, or rock above; in this room you can nearly walk upright. Our candles burning well we felt no danger from the air; we found abundance of bats hanging in a torpid state to the roof of the rooms; some of these we brought out, and it being in the spring of the year, they soon revived. Finding that our cord was almost out, which was about sixty yards long, and being much fatigued and very warm, occasioned by our exertions, we returned to its mouth again, satisfied that we had all got out in safety. This cavern appeared to me to have been formed by a general rent of the hill, for we could in some places see for ten feet in the openings of the rock, which were filled with stones evidently scaled off in the general fracture of the mountain. It is evident that this cavern has been the refuge of wild beasts, from the number of bones it contains.

* * * * * * *

Immediately above the mouth of this [Dunlap's] creek is a small village called Bridgeport; it is however considered as a part of Brownsville, on the other side of the creek, divided only by a bridge over its mouth. Up this creek are some of our best merchant mills, which manufacture vast quantities of flour for the New Orleans trade."

He expands the description of

"BROWNSVILLE
(Formerly called Redstone Old Fort)
This town is handsomely situated on the E. side of the river . . . it contains with Bridgeport about ninety houses, fifteen mercantile stores, one rope walk, a considerable boatyard, factories of earthen ware, nails, scythes, sickles, &c. The inhabitants are industrious and healthy, and the neighborhood around, being the first settled in the western country, is rich and well cultivated. It is in Fayette county, Pennsylvania, and twelve miles from Union[town] or Beasontown, the seat of justice for that county. This last town is

also situated in a rich and fine settlement, contains about a hundred and ten houses, and twenty mercantile stores; at the west end of the town are two valuable grist-mills, on a branch of Redstone creek, and in the neighborhood are several furnaces and forges.

In Brownsville, on the point of the upper bank, are the remains of an old fort, within which, and a considerable distance below the surface, are yet to be found human bones of a very large size; and if I mistake not, I was lately told by a respectable citizen of the place, that in digging a hole for a necessary, he had discovered a skeleton in a kind of box coffin. These relicks, no doubt, were deposited here during the long and bloody war with the Indians, in the earlier settlement of the country. By land, it is thirty-two miles from Pittsburgh, on the direct road from Philadelphia to Washington, Pa., and is well known to migrators as a place of embarkation [on flatboats down the Monongahela and Ohio Rivers.]

Within about a mile of this place, I lately visited a curious [pictograph] rock, on the face of which is engraved an irregular circle nearly meeting; at about ten or twelve inches distant from each other, holes to the amount of seven or eight were made on the ring and something deeper and larger; and facing the opening in the circle, about six inches distant from it, is engraved a man's head, apparently of large size. This carving is recollected as one of the first curiosities of the country. The rock lying level with the surface, we had considerable trouble to clean it of dirt and leaves in order to see plainly the form of the carving, and to trace, if possible, the intention of the artist; this, however, remains yet to be found out."

One mile downriver, at Redstone creek, "several valuable grist, saw, and oil mills, and three miles up it is a paper-mill, owned by Jackson and Sharpless; it makes about fifteen thousand dollars worth of paper annually, and it is altogether incapable of supplying such quantities as the country demands."

WILLIAMSPORT [Monongahela]

is described as a "small but growing village," rather than a town; and

ELIZABETHTOWN [Elizabeth]

is a "small village, but the inhabitants do much in boatbuilding business. The ships Monongahela Farmer and the Ann Jean [*Anna Jane*] were built here."

M'KEESPORT is:

"a small village . . . [with] several mercantile stores, and a large brew-house, this however does little business . . . . The town takes its name from the proprietor, John M'Kee."

"Perrystown, or Turtle creek [North Braddock]" is 5 miles downriver [actually 4] and "This town lies just above the mouth of the creek [and] it contains but a few homes, and very little business of any kind is as yet done here."

The site of Braddock's defeat is three miles downriver per Cramer [it's actually 1.5 miles] and "This place is rendered famous on account of general Braddock's having met here with a defeat in an engagement with the Indians and French [on July 9, 1755.] He received a mortal wound himself, and his men were wonderfully cut to pieces; this was much attributed to his refusing them the privilege of fighting as their enemies fought, in ambush. Bones of the dead are still to be found on the ground, and are not infrequently plowed up. A brass piece [of artillery], it is said, may be sometimes seen in a very deep hole in the river, opposite the field of battle. The trees on the side of the hill still bear the marks of the balls that were discharged during the engagement."

* * * * * * *

'OF THE ALLEGHENY . . .
including the portage from Erie, (Presqu' Isle):

This town is handsomely situated on the south bank of lake Erie, opposite a peninsula which runs down the lake for a considerable distance, forming between it and the town a handsome harbour for the mooring of vessels, this however is somewhat difficult to enter . . . . It is the seat of justice for Erie county, Pa. The old fort just below the town and which contains the venerable remains of general ['Mad Anthony'] Wayne, is principally evacuated.[1] The town is by land one hundred and twenty-five miles, in nearly a due north direction, from Pittsburgh."

Additional information
about WATERFORD (LeBoeuf) is:

"This town is situated on French creek, and at the head of water communication between it and Erie; a garrison was formerly kept here, it is now nearly destroyed; it has a post-office and several mercantile stores and ware-houses. Between this place and Erie a turnpike road is about to be completed, to render more easy and cheap the transportation of goods, wares, &c. It is in Erie county."

The information concerning MEADVILLE is unchanged; however,

FRANKLIN progressed "but slowly." And, "The French formerly kept a garrison here, which is now destroyed, but is said to have buried in it a brass piece of considerable value."

---

[1]A Revolutionary War hero, Wayne defeated a coalition of Native American tribes at the battle of Fallen Timbers, near present-day Toledo, O., in 1794. He then negotiated the Treaty of Greenville which forced the tribes to cede most of the territory in the Northwest between Lake Erie and the Ohio River. This led to the immediate movement of whites into the region. In 1809, his body was disinterred and relocated to the family plot in St. David's Episcopal Church Cemetery in Radnor, Pa.

FREEPORT is designated a village, rather than a town!

* * * * * * *

More "OF THE OHIO" includes:

"BEAVER, (formerly called M'Intosh.)

This town lies on a very high bank . . . contains several mercantile stores, and from its situation must in time become a place of considerable business. From the great depth to water, the citizens have been obliged to introduce through pipes the water of a spring on the side of a hill about a quarter of a mile back of the town."

GEORGETOWN

contained "three mercantile stores, and but a few houses, has a post-office, and adjacent to it are some valuable gristmills."

∾

— 4 —

THE NAVIGATOR, 1808

This sixth edition included data on "THE MISSOURI AND COLUMBIA RIVERS, as discovered by the voyage under captains Lewis and Clark."

In "PITTSBURGH . . .

The appearance of the ditch and mound, [of Ft. DuQuesne] with its salient angles and bastions are still to be seen.

On the margin of the Allegheny and near to the old fort stood a row of houses, tolerably elegant and neat, but have been swept away in the course of time, some by the encroachments of the floods, and others were torn down for the purpose of forming an opening to the river from the garrison. Not a trace of those buildings now remain, except some of the stones used in their foundation, which may yet be seen jutting out of the bank as the earth caves into the river.

There stood at the point, as late as 1784, a large umbrageous tree – its fate too has been unfortunate – the floods undermined the ground and it was swept away.

On part of this ground now stands a large brewery, and two dwellings; the situation is too low indeed for a general building, and the bank too subject to cavings. – Just above Fort DuQuesne, is the remains of the garrison built by general Stanwix, called Fort Pitt . . . and is said to have cost the British nation 60,000 L. Sterling, about $266,666.66. The bricks which composed the walls of this garrison, have been applied to building houses, which are distinguishable from the rest of the brick houses in town by the whiteness of the colour impressed on them by the strength of the lime and cement used in their application.

Within the embankment are still some of its barracks and a strong stone powder magazine, the only remains of the British buildings; there are also a few dwellings built within three or four years. – The British officers, commanding this garrison, had, on the bank of the Allegheny [River], most elegant gardens; near to these they planted an orchard of excellent bearing apple trees, some of which still bear fruit, others have been swept away by the surly floods of the river, and others cut down to give room for building.

Fort Pitt . . . now makes a part of the town of Pittsburgh, though its banks and ditches form a considerable obstruction to its being regularly built on, and very much spoil the beauty of the view from the head of Liberty and Penn streets to the Monongahela river.

Fort Fayette, the present garrison . . . is also within the borough . . . on the Allegheny. It answers as a place of deposit, and for the convenience of stationing soldiers destined down the Ohio, and Mississippi; as a place of defence it is useless.

In the year 1760, a small town, called Pittsburgh, was built near Fort Pitt, and about 200 families resided in it; but upon the Indian [Pontiac's 'Conspiracy'] war breaking out in May 1763, they abandoned their homes and retired into the Fort.

The bottom or the plain on which Pittsburgh stands, would seem, from the circumstances to have been made ground, and the Allegheny river to have one washed the base of Grant's hill; but through time and accident, found it way by some progressions, from that hill to its present bed.

. . . There are two rises, or what are called first and second banks, running parallel with that river, which would seem to have once formed its Eastern origin. These elevations make beautiful situations for either gardens or buildings. – In digging wells in the town, the various kinds of sand and gravel are found as appear on the beaches and in the beds of the rivers; pieces of wood and strata of dirt and leaves are also frequently discovered eight or ten feet below the surface. The Allegheny is now working itself back again. It has washed away about 50 or 60 feet of ground on its eastern bank within 30 years.

This plain which is of a rich sandy loam, is about half a mile in width from the Allegheny to the point of Grant's hill, its widest part; thence up that river it gets narrower, until about four miles, where the hill closes to the river bank. But the town may extend as far as the Two Mile run; the bottom that distance is spacious, and well calculated for building on. It is now enclosed in orchards, meadows and grain fields, and produces fine crops of each.

The present town of Pittsburgh was first laid out in the year 1765; it was afterwards laid and surveyed in May, 1784, by Col. George Woods, by order of Tench Francis, Esq. Attorney for John Penn, Jun[ior]. and John Penn. The beauty and very commanding situation of the place has increased its buildings, population and business, beyond all calculations. It now contains about 500 dwellings, the greater number perhaps wood, some stone, and many elegantly built with brick, two and three stories high. The public buildings are: A large and spacious court house handsomely built with brick; a large brick market house; . . . a stone jail; a bank, established here January 1, 1804; . . . a large stone house on the bank of the Monongahela, four stories high, built by the [Oliver] Evans's of Philadelphia, for a steam grist and paper mill, not yet in motion" and five large churches.

After a long descriptive statement on Pittsburgh's industry, he notes that "On entering the town, the stranger is rather offended with its dark and heavy appearance. This arises from the smoke of the coal, which is used as the common fuel; and of which about 170,000 bushels are consumed annually. It costs six cents a bushel at your door . . . . Our rough hills are filled with it, and our rooms in winter feel the effects of its warmth, and cheerfulness. Wood as an article of fuel costs 2 dollars a cord delivered. The abundance and cheapness of coal, will be peculiarly advantageous to Pittsburgh in her progress in arts and manufactures. Coal Hill, on the south side of the Monongahela, abounds in coal; and a pit in it is said to have taken fire about the year 1765, and continued burning for 8 years; and another pit on Pike run, which burned for 10 years. This is a high and steep hill, and its top affords a handsome prospect of the town and rivers below it.

From the immense quantity of coal burnt, there arises a cloud of smoke which hangs over the town in a body, and may be seen at two or three miles distance; when in the town, this cloud of smoke is not discovered, and the place soon becomes familiar to the eye, while the ear is occupied with the mixed sounds of the implements of industry, from 4 o'clock in the morning till 10 at night."

* * * * * * *

Up the Monongahela,
CLARKSBURGH is a new town.

It "stands on the E. side of the [West Fork] river, 40 miles S. E. of Morgantown, is the chief town of Harrison Co., Virginia, and contains 50 houses, a court house and jail."

MORGANTOWN

is now listed as being "305 miles from Philadelphia, and above 63 by land above [or North to] Pittsburgh."

"Albert GALLATIN, Esq., Secretary of the U. S. Treasury," is identified as the owner of the glassworks at NEW GENEVA, "and [is] now conducted by Mr. [James W.] Nicholson his partner."

Within a few miles of FREDERICKTOWN "is a large brewery and distillery, and tanyard."

BRIDGEPORT

Has "several mercantile stores, an earthen pottery, tanyard, a wire weaver, card maker, hatters, a boat yard, and a market house. It contains 56 dwellings."

BROWNSVILLE

now " contains 120 houses, principally of wood, some handsomely built of stone and brick . . . eighteen mercantile stores, numerous industries . . . two boatyards . . . and one printing office which issues a weekly paper.

WILLIAMSPORT (Monongahela)

" . . . is a growing village . . . 20 miles east of Washington, and about 23 above Pittsburgh. [actually 32 miles] –

The inhabitants have been petitioning the legislature for the privilege of forming it into a new County, by taking off a part of Washington, Westmoreland, Fayette, and Allegheny Counties, all of which corner near that place. It is said 4000 dollars have been already subscribed to meet part of the expences of County buildings, &c."

ELIZABETHTOWN is

eighteen miles [actually 23] above Pittsburgh, "The town does not thrive much. Original proprietor, Col. Stephen Bayard."

M'KEESPORT is

"A small and dull village...12 miles [actually 15.5] above Pittsburgh."

* * * * * * *

"OF THE ALLEGHENY
ERIE (PRESQU'ISLE)

The country in its vicinity is settling rapidly; and the trade in salt [from New York], of which there are about 7000 or 8000 barrels enter that port annually, is increasing. The convenience of the turnpike road now erecting between Erie and Waterford, a portage of fifteen miles, will be very considerable when completed.

Erie has a post office, several mercantile stores, and public inns, and a number of the mechanical branches are carried on with spirit. The town is well supplied with fish from the lake, and cranberries from the Peninsula, of which many barrels are sold at the Pittsburgh market yearly."

The data for Waterford, Franklin, and Freeport are unchanged; however,

"MEADVILLE

has a post and printing office which issues a weekly paper . . . . It has a well regulated school, a fixed minister, and a society for the encouragement of home manufactures."

* * * * * * *

Down the OHIO RIVER
"BEAVER (formerly FORT M'INTOSH) . . .

was laid out in 1797-8, and probably would have had a fairer prospect of rising to some importance had it been built at the mouth of the creek. . . . Beaver has about 30 scattered houses in it, a stone jail, a post office, 4 mercantile stores, several public inns, a printing office which issues a weekly paper, and is the seat of justice for Beaver co."

GEORGETOWN is now identified as a "small village."

∽

— 5 —

Pittsburgh Gazette, November 16, 1810
FLOOD

"On Sunday the 11th inst. the Monongahela and Allegheny rivers, rose suddenly to a height not recollected by the oldest settlers. We are not able to ascertain the damage done on this occasion; but in this place and its vicinity it was considerable – all the property on the Allegheny has suffered more or less – the large Wharf at Fort Fayette was entirely swept away – a valuable brick house the property of Mr. William Anderson was greatly injured, the cellars all filled, the gardens, and brick kilns damaged – all the bottoms within several miles were under water, and the loss in Grain, Cattle, Feed[?] and Bridges must amount to many thousands of dollars – the western part of the Borough, below Liberty Street was nearly insulated; the two Rivers wanted but a few inches of joining, where Liberty and Market streets meet – this melancholy occasion afforded one instance of consolation – a beautiful new brig, the property of Mr. Brintnal Robbins came down the Allegheny, and anchored opposite the town – She moved down the Ohio on Wednesday, bound for New Orleans."[1]

ℒ

— 6 —

Pittsburgh Morning Post, November 23, 1858
"LOCAL AFFAIRS
Pittsburgh Forty [Three] Years Ago [in 1815]

A friend has furnished us with a copy of the old Directory of the Borough of Pittsburgh, published in 1815. It contains ninety-four pages of the names of the then residents, most of whom it is scarcely necessary to say, have passed away. Besides this there [is] an appendix containing a variety of statistical information of an interesting character. Even at that early day Pittsburgh had made such progress in manufactures and mechanical arts that she claimed the title of 'The Birmingham of America'– a title which our present rich and flourishing city, with it daily augmenting commerce and manufacturing, still boasts with a just pride.

A mere mention of some of the names and facts contained in this little book will serve to recall interesting reminiscences to a large class of our readers.

---

[1]Pittsburgh's population? 4,740.

48

In 1815, Ephraim Pentland was Prothonotary, Sam. Jones, Register and Recorder, and Wm. Woods, Sheriff of the county. Samuel Roberts was resident Judge of the Court of Common Pleas, and Francis M'Clure and George Robinson his Associates. John Darragh and Philip Mowry were the leading Justices of the Peace, and Samuel Hubley, Wm. Murdoch and the Inevitable John Smith, were Constables. John M. Snowden was the President of the Town Council, Lazarus Stewart, Town Clerk, and John B. Gray, High Constable.

In 1815, the eastern and western mail arrived three times a week, and mails from Beaver, Steubenville, Erie, and such like places, once a week only. The rates of postage were from twelve cents for 40 miles to thirty-seven and a half for 500. The population of Pittsburgh was then 9,431 . . . . In that year there were 35 slaves in the county, but only one in the city."[1]

Taxes were then imposed on various goods and merchandize manufactured within the United States. For instance, pig iron was taxed $1 per ton; castings $1.50 per ton; nails 1 cent per pound; tallow candles 3 cents per pound; hats and caps 8 per cent advalorem; playing cards 50 per cent, advalorem; manufactured tobacco 20 per cent, advalorem; leather 5 per cent. Liquor was taxed 25 cents on the gallon on the quantity distilled; household furniture, carriages, watches, &c., were all highly taxed. These rates of taxation would astonish people in our days.

At that time the venerable William Wilkins was President of the Bank of Pittsburgh, and Alex. Johnson, Jr.,

---

[1]The Pennsylvania legislature abolished slavery on May 1, 1780, gradually. All slaves, on that date, would remain slaves if registered; those born after that date would be freed at the age of twenty-eight!

Note: Pittsburgh was incorporated as a city in 1816.

Cashier. Judge Wilkins was also President of the Pittsburgh and Greensburg Turnpike Company, the Vigilant Fire Company, and several other useful public institutions.

The list of the streets in the borough occupies the half of a very small page printed with large type. Now their name is legion.

The manufacturing business of Pittsburgh at that day consisted of a steam-engine factory; an air foundry; an anvil and anchor factory; a brass foundry; a butt hinge factory; three large breweries (the fathers of the city loved good ale as well as their sons); two lead factories; three rope walks, at which the principal part of the cordage for [Commodore Oliver Hazard] Perry's fleet [on Lake Erie during the 'War of 1812'] was made; five glass houses; a woolen factory; a pottery; a lock factory, and the usual number of small mechanical establishments.

This was the day of small things. Now our manufactories of iron, and glass, and other useful products are multiplied an hundred fold. The product of several of our establishments now is greater annually than the combined products of all the establishments in the city was forty years ago; and our resources are such that the next two score years will undoubtedly result in a still more wonderful advancement of the manufacturing interests of our city than the last have."

Brownsville *American Telegraph*, October 30, 1816
"For the *Telegraph*.
PERRYOPOLIS

This village is delightfully situated between the navigable waters of the Monongahela and Youghagany [Youghiogheny Rivers] near the bank of the latter [in Fayette County on present-day Route 51 a few miles south of I-70.] A few months ago where nothing was to be seen but a solitary mansion house, a badly cultivated farm and an open grove, we now behold a flourishing town, on a beautiful eminence, gradually and uniformly declining from the center; and active industry every where plying her busy hands. On the 14th of January 1814, the first lots were sold at public auction. Some were sold for less than 20 dollars, which at this time command a price which at one surprises and pleases the candid and discerning mind. It was not until the June following that any purchaser had the courage and enterprise to raise a single building in the place; then that industrious and good citizen, John Ebhert, erected a frame on lot No. 16. Since that time the progress of improvement and population has been exceedingly rapid. About fifty dwelling houses have been built, and many more are building. If these be not large, they are generally decent, economical and commodious, formed of good materials and the workmanship is by no means disreputable, to the mechanics who have been employed.

The buildings which have been erected for the manufacture of green glass are equal, it is believed, to any in the United States. The factory is owned by twenty three reputable citizens, mostly of Washington township, and all of Fayette county. If wealth, industry and perseverance can command success, this company must be successful. When it is considered that a capital of more than twenty thousand dollars had been expended, that a large stock of glass had already been manufactured, it is pitiful, indeed, to see how sanctimoniously some men will hesitate to give credit to their promissory bills now in circulation. It is asserted without fear of contradiction that about $2000 only have been issued. Can any person divine why a company so strong in its funds, so honourable in its members, so attentive to business, successful in its operations, prosecuting a factory of extensive public utility should not be entitled to a credit to the amount of one tenth part of the stock actually expended, when other institutions, merely speculative, whose object has been monopoly and exclusive privilege, pursuing extravagant schemes of agrandizement, and issuing paper probably to three times the amount of capital, are patronized and encouraged without scruple? Correct information once diffused among the people on this subject must effectually revolutionize their views and feelings.

The window glass and porter bottles made at this factory are of quality equal to any in America.

There is also a Flint Glass Factory just completed and [is] commencing its operations, at the westerly side of town. These works are owned by Dr. Thomas Hersey, a principal proprietor of the original survey of the town, by Capt. S. Miller, Mr. Ayres Lyon, and Andrew Lyon, Esq. This institution has been erected at great expense and is on respectable footing. It is well supplied with ingenious workmen and there is nothing to hinder its prosperity which human wisdom can foresee. The enterprise, industry and economy everywhere visible to every stage of this institution must be pleasing to every good citizen.

A scheme has been projected and is now carrying into effect to establish a Bank upon a new and improved plan . . . .

The Banking house is now erecting in an expeditious a manner as possible. It will be an elegant, strong and convenient stone building, on the south side of [lot] No. 12. This site for the bank has been gratuitously bestowed by Dr. Hersey for the benefit of the institution.

In this place there are persons residing of various denominations, but there is not, as yet, any convenient place of public worship.

We have, at this time, four mercantile stores, well filled and doing a good share of business; but the future greatness of this place, or any other town in the interior of our country, depends on the establishment of suitable factories and industrious citizens who will draw the circulating medium to them, and on the speculations of the money draining merchants, who are carrying away all our cash from us as fast as they can get it into their possession.

Perryopolis is surrounded by a numerous and wealthy population. The adjacent country is noticed by travelers for salubrity of air and fertility of soil. The town itself stands on one of the most healthful situations in the world. Its well furnished the best water. The plan of its survey is original, it gives an opportunity for a free ventilation and leaves every part accessible and convenient for business. Saw mills and grist mills are numerous and at a convenient distance from the town. Steam works of every description might, it is believed, be built with a prospect of good profit to the owner.

To give a minute account of the various kinds of works, shop, &c. would extend my present limits. Suffice it to say, that in proportion to the number of inhabitants we are well accommodated with mechanics and more are constantly settling among us. Arrangements are making for opening roads and for obtaining a post office in this and several other towns on the route between Uniontown and Pittsburgh. Petitions out immediately to be prepared and presented to the Legislature of Pennsylvania as soon as they are in session, for opening and improving a state road, and for making the Monongahela and Youghagany navigable.

It is obvious to all that the name of Perryopolis was given to the town in commemoration of [Oliver Hazard] Perry, the [War of 1812] hero of the [Battle of] Lake [Erie in 1813], and it is hoped, that it will eventually be an honorable monument to his memory.

A VILLAGER"

ᴂ

— 8 —

Pittsburgh Gazette, February 5, 1819

This is a satiric critique of the new National Road, which had been completed from Cumberland, Md., via Brownsville, to Wheeling, Va., in 1818, by-passing Pittsburgh.

"MEMORANDUM OF A LATE TOUR INTO OHIO

Arrival at Washington [Pa.]; pretty situated on a hill. Mem.[orandum] always to enter Washington when there is no ice on the streets. Washington [is] going to be a great place on account of the national turnpike; heard two well dressed men at the Globe tavern, over a gill of Clark's best [ale?], say, 'farewell Pittsburgh! [the] turnpike has put your pretensions to rest – we shall rise on your ruins!' Being much alarmed for some of my friends at Pitt, I presumed to ask the gentlemen 'how we were ruined?' One of them turned full upon me and answered, 'why , sir, you will lose the carrying trade – don't you know Wheeling is to be the place of departure for boats in [the] future?', but quothe I, timidly and trembling for the fate of old Fort Pitt our manufactures. – 'A fig for your manufactures,' exclaimed the other gentleman, 'we will knock you in there too; have we not got stone coal as well as you?' Mem[orandum] – to write back to Pittsburgh to advise our manufacturers to sell and come to Washington – great place, and it is generally supposed that the national road will tend very much to sharpen the wit of college students [at Washington College].

Left Washington in deep distress about 'dear sooty Pittsburgh,' breakfast in Claysville, another promising town; unfortunately for 'mine host,' the Cumberland road was maliciously located on the back side of his house; an awkward dilemma; advised him to make application for an <u>appropriation</u> for a <u>cross</u> turnpike <u>round</u> his house; asked the landlord who the town was called for, the man got mad and said that I was quizzing – Mem[orandum]. – Not to make so free again with the landlords of the turnpike. West Alexandria; Hardscrabble – thriving place, property rising; landlord and blacksmith disputing about the price of a lot; one said it had been proposed to him at 5,000 dollars, the other declared he would not look at less than 6,000. Wonderful magic of the Cumberland road! Wheeling creek; 4 splendid, unfinished bridges, to cost government 40,000. Quere – when will they be finished and who is to pay for them?

Wheeling, most promising town I have seen; this, I was told was to be a future place of deposit for all western goods; the manufactures of Pittsburgh were to be moved here. Quere – what will the good people of Washington say to this arrangement? Mem[orandum]. – There appears to be one defect in the situation of Wheeling; there seems to be one place to build houses, on account of the river on one side, and a hill on the other.- Suppose, however, this difficulty can be <u>removed</u> by the government . . . . [Hiatus]"

He continued his commentary into Ohio, much of which is illegible.

∾

— 9 —

Pittsburgh Gazette, July 22, 1825
"From the *Erie Gazette*
A SKETCH OF ERIE

'What a beautiful place!' is the language which we every day hear applied to our village by the sojourning stranger: -- All pronounce it beautiful, and many view it with the most enthusiastic admiration.

As it is becoming common for fashionable and intelligent strangers traveling to the Atlantic coast, to make the tour by the way of Erie, it may not be unacceptable to the public to have a sketch of a place which has lately attracted so much attention.

The town is situated directly on the bank of Lake Erie, where it forms the beautiful harbor of Presque Isle. The bay or harbor is about four miles in length, and a mile and a half in breadth. On the north and east of the town there is a grand and boundless view of water. On the north and west the eve is relieved by the peninsula which makes the bay. The banks of the Lake at Erie, are about sixty feet high, and the country rises gently for ten or twelve miles back, which is the summit level between the waters of the Lake and the Allegheny river. The town is laid out on the plan of the city of Philadelphia, all the streets intersecting each other at right angles; no streets less than sixty feet wide, and the principal ones one hundred feet. It contains from eight hundred to one thousand inhabitants, and its population is rapidly increasing – I can safely venture the assertion, that there is no city in the Union which exhibits a lovelier scenery, or combines more natural beauties, than the town of Erie, and the fineness of its climate, and the health of its air, have long been proverbial. The soil of Erie county is of the generous and productive kind, which makes the husbandman, 'bearing his sheaves, rejoice.'

Travellers, especially those from the direction of Pittsburgh, have frequently expressed their surprise at the fineness of the roads, and the facilities of traveling through a country which they had heretofore considered as an almost impenetrable forest. Indeed, at present, travelers have every thing to invite them in this direction. Do they travel for cheapness and expedition? It has been truly said that a man could not afford to walk from this place to New York – it would cost him more than to go in a post coach. Is a man's object to improve his health? The breezes of the Lake 'carry healing in their wings.' Does he wish to behold the beauties and sublimities of nature? The scenery of the Lakes and the falls of Niagara surpass his expectations. Does he wish to view the most stupendous work of human art? The New York [Erie] canal fulfils his wish. It may be proper to add, that the facilities of traveling are every day increasing. The different lines of stages are making great improvements, and a steam boat is now building at this place, for the express purpose of accommodating travelers between this and Buffalo."

"PITTSBURGH in the year Eighteen Hundred and Twenty-six,
containing SKETCHES TOPOGRAPICAL, HISTORICAL AND STATISTICAL; TOGETHER WITH A DIRECTORY OF THE CITY, AND A VIEW OF ITS VARIOUS MANUFACTURES, POPULATION, IMPROVEMENTS, &c . . . BY S[amuel]. JONES."

His description of the Pittsburgh area is far different from Cramer's 1802 version.

"The city has four unequal sides, but is very nearly a regular right angle triangle; the side bordering on the Allegheny being the longest, and the line from one river to the other, on the East side, the shortest of the three. The longest side is nearly a mile, and the shortest, nearly three quarters of a mile. The principal streets join the Monongahela at right angles, and these are intersected nearly at right angles by others running parallel to the Monongahela. On the North, or rather North-western side of these, are two ranges of squares parallel with the Allegheny, which, of course, join the other streets and squares at irregular angles."

". . . The highest altitude of this [Coal] Hill (nearly opposite Ferry street) is 465 feet. It extends, unbroken, for several miles up and down the river. In that part of the hill above the Pittsburgh Glassworks, and near it summit, there has been fire burning for many years, and the smoke may be seen daily curling from out [of] the fissures of the rocks.

. . . On the back or Eastern part of the city, are Grant's and Boyd's Hills. – The first is within the precincts, and is partly in a state of lawn; its height is only about 7 feet. The second, is one the boundary line; commencing its rise not far from the Monongahela, along which it soon extends for about two miles; one mile of which is composed of rocky and perpendicular precipices of a hundred feet in height. – From the summits of these, it slopes gradually towards Grant's Hill, forming a small, but beautiful belt of land, which is devoted to small farms and summer residences. On the North-east part of the city, and adjoining Grant's Hill, where it rises with a gradual ascent, is Quarry Hill, whence the principal part of all the stone used in Pittsburgh has been taken – from its point, which is just within the city, it extends along and binds the second flat of the Allegheny, for about two miles, when it is broken by the ravine of the two-mile run. The aspect of this Hill on the West side, is very barren and poor, presenting scarcely any thing else than stone quarries. The top and opposite side is composed of a tolerable good soil, but is poorly cultivated. Here are a great number of coal pits. The highest elevation of Quarry Hill is about 440 feet. On the Western side of the Allegheny, opposite the lower part of the city, is an abrupt promontory, called Hogback Hill, from its peculiar formation. It is about half a mile in length, and is of little value. In the rear of this hill, and running North and South, is the great chain of hills that bind the flat lands on the Allegheny and the Ohio.

In all these elevations, coal is found in immense quantities – except in Grant's, Boyd's, and Hogback hills; their altitude not being sufficient to bring them within the range of the great strata of that mineral which pervades this region of country.

Pittsburgh has several suburban villages, that contribute to, and are supplied from the great centre, with which their strength and prosperity are intimately connected.

On, or nearly adjoining the North-eastern boundary of the city, and on the flat between Quarry Hill and the Allegheny river, the NORTHERN LIBERTIES are situated, and

PITTSBURGH ABOUT 1825: From an old dinner plate, made by
Clews of Staffordshire, England.
Source: Sarah H. Killikelly, *The History of Pittsburgh*
(Pittsburgh: B. C. & Gordon Montgomery Co., 1906).

are intended as a continuation of Pittsburgh. They were laid
out in 1816, by Geo. A. Bayard and James Adams. The lots
were originally let on perpetual leases, and such was the ea-
gerness of persons to obtain property at that time, that from
one and a half to two dollars per foot were readily given.
However, the consequences of the peace [of the War of
1812] – the ruinous policy of the banking system, at that
time in vogue, and the numerous train of evils which ever
follow a depression of enterprise, rendered many of the
leasees unable to pay their rents, notwithstanding many of
them had put up comfortable habitations. The proprietors
were, therefore, obliged to take back many of their lots. Yet
the village has lost none of its population as to numbers – it

is now improving rapidly, and contains the Phoenix Cotton Factory, Juniata Iron Works, &c.

Adjoining the South-eastern boundary of the city, on the Monongahela, stands KENSINGTON, or as it is commonly called, Pipe-town; deriving this name through one of its early settlers, an eccentric little gentleman, still well known among all classes, for his odd humour, and the universality of his mechanical genius, Mr. William Price, who established the Pipe manufactory there. Kensington is composed of lots laid out by several individuals, which run from the road, or extension of Second street, to the river – and to every one it presents matter of surprise, how so ungainly a situation should be thought of, not only for private dwellings, but for extensive manufactories, as there is not, if we except the lower corner, on Suke's Run, naturally, thirty feet square of level ground, in the whole place – Yet, there are here, two steam rolling mills, a wire manufactory, an air foundry, a stream grist-mill, a steam engine for turning and grinding brass and iron, and a brewery.

A short distance above Kensington, on the South and opposite side of the [Monongahela] river, stands BIRMINGHAM, and SIDNEYVILLE, which may be considered the southern suburb of Pittsburgh. The villages were laid out by Dr. Nathaniel Bedford and Mr. Isaac Gregg. The name of Sidneyville, however, has been lost in that of Birmingham; as the latter is now applied to both. For several years after the location of these villages, which was in 1811, they increased quite rapidly, but latterly, their increase has been very gradual. It is here that the well known Birmingham Glass is manufactured . . . . By an Act of the late Legislature, Birmingham was incorporated into a borough.

On the western side of the Allegheny, on the second bottom, a few hundred yards from the shore, it the TOWN OF ALLEGHENY. This place was laid out by order of the Supreme Executive Council of Pennsylvania, in 1789.[1] It is an exact square, and consists only of a hundred in-lots, 60 by 240 feet. The out-lots, however, are very numerous, containing from eight to ten acres each – they extend a considerable distance up from the Allegheny, and down the Ohio about two miles and a half, embracing the several thousand acres, which were denominated the RESERVED TRACT [for veterans of the Revolution.] The town is connected with Pittsburgh, by the Allegheny bridge, and is a great thoroughfare, as here, all the principal highways, leading to and from the North and West, concentrate. It is here also, that the Western Penitentiary of Pennsylvania, is erected, which for workmanship and excellence of design, is not surpassed by any building of the kind in the United States. The form is that of an octagon, enclosing an area about two acres and three-fourths. The main, or front building, is 122 feet in length, and 46 feet high, and flanked by two circular towers, all surmounted with battlements. . . . The establishment will have cost, when completed, about 130,000 dollars.

Two miles above Pittsburgh, on the Eastern shore of the Allegheny, is the village of LAWRENCEVILLE; laid out in the year 1815, by William B. Foster. – Its commencement and progress were identified with the erection of the U. S. Arsenal, which is located on a strip of land, running from the river, and occupying the center of the village. The population, amounting to nearly 200, are principally engaged about the public works. The Arsenal and buildings connected with

---

[1]Allegheny was to be the designated county seat in the newly surveyed Reserve Tract in Allegheny County in 1788. Allegheny was laid out in 1790. However, in 1791, the "people of Pittsburgh" petitioned the legislature and it rescinded that provision. Pittsburgh's population in 1790 was ca. 376. Rooms had to be rented for the "court house and gaol." Allegheny was incorporated as a borough in 1826.

it, form an elegant group, and were built under the superintendence of Major A.R. Woolley. The mounting of ordnance, and the making and repairing of various arms and military accouterments, are the entire employments of the artisans engaged or enlisted. There are, at present, a company of artillerist stationed here, and the whole is under the command of Major Churchill.

But to return to the city – Its appearance is far from being prepossessing; the everlasting cloud of smoke that hovers over it, and the black and sooty countenance of [eve]ry thing, animate and inanimate, render it not unlike an immense smith-shop. The houses are without any kind of regularity; on one square may be seen a handsome block of brick buildings, occupied by merchants and private families, while, on the next, is a row of one and two story frames, some with their sides, and others with their gable ends on the street, exhibiting a motley assemblage of cordwainers, small dealers, and no small number of those interesting places of refreshments, termed grocery and liquor stores. Nearly the whole town is built in this way. Why it is so, cannot be explained, unless it be said that it was intended to realize a line of the old song –

'Variety is charming.'

Of late years, great improvements have been made by paving those streets, that were formerly deep and dirty. Paved side-walks are very general throughout, and as the city progresses, attention to various objects of utility, connected with cleanliness, will, doubtless be paid. The completion of the contemplated Water Works, will be of immense advantage, not only in cases of fire, or private convenience, but in cleansing the streets and pavements, and in the summer, rendering the city cool and less dusty . . . with a hundred roads leading towards her, through her great highways, is always filled with a numerous concourse of strangers, of all classes, countries, and denominations. The spring and fall, however, are the most busy periods; yet, at all times, the city exhibits great bustle and activity; the rattling of drays, carts and wagons; the puffing of stream; the noise of machinery, and the continued tread of the passing multitude, indicate the industry and extensive business of the place.

In matters of taste, in relation to their public and private buildings, the Pittsburghers have but little to boast. The Episcopal Church . . . is by far the handsomest edifice in the city. The others are very ordinary and common place, being built more for cheapness than ornament. As to literary institutions, if we except the Medical Society, and the Apprentices' Library Association, there are none."[2]

ও

---

[2]Northern Liberties, a borough in 1829, was annexed by Pittsburgh in 1837. Lawrenceville, a borough in 1837, was annexed in 1868, and Birmingham, a borough in 1826, in 1872.

— 11 —
"Pittsburgh Gazette,
May 14, 1830
[Wheeling again!]

The citizens of Pittsburgh consider that they have much reason to complain of the editors of newspapers in Baltimore, in relation to their annunciations of the stage of water in the Ohio. – The papers of this city and Wheeling regularly announce the height of the water; the Baltimore paper as regularly copy the statements from the Wheeling papers, but entirely and perseveringly [without?] noticing the Pittsburgh accounts. A western merchant in Baltimore, if he were to judge only from the papers printed there, might suppose that the Ohio was dry, or that it sprung from a subterranean channel just above Wheeling.

If it is convenient to publish the stage of water only at one place, surely, for the information of those interested, the *higher* point should be preferred, for this simple and obvious reason – while steam boats can come to and depart from Pittsburgh, they must at least pass by Wheeling.

We are induced to make these remarks, and we do it in haste, while the compositor is waiting on us, because a gentleman, direct from Baltimore, has just stated that he had paid twenty-five cents per hundred more for carriage to Wheeling, than was asked to this place, under the impression that steam boats could not come to Pittsburgh. How true his supposition was, may be known by looking at our Steam Boat List for the present week, which shows no less than fifteen arrivals and fourteen departures.

But as a farther evidence of the navigableness of the river, we will state that it is now just eighty days since navigation commenced, and in that time we have had 183 arrivals and 190 departures. It is true that Wheeling can exhibit a much longer list of arrivals and departures, because every boat which comes to this place from below, will add both an arrival and departure to the Wheeling list, if she should only land a deck passenger or a bacon ham at that place.

We cannot believe the suggestion of some of our citizens, that the commission merchants in Wheeling pay the editors of newspapers in Baltimore for publishing the account of the stage of water at Wheeling. We believe this preference of the *lower* point, in their account of the stage of water in the Ohio, arises from inadvertence, and we trust it will be corrected.

We will only add, for the information of those concerned, that the tonnage of steam boats of light draft, now exceeds the whole amount of tonnage engaged in the Pittsburgh trade three years ago."

PITTSBURGH IN 1830.
Source: *Fleming's Views of Old Pittsburgh.*

Pittsburgh Gazette, February 14, 1832

"The Inundation

The last three months has been an almost unprecedented period. Our winter commenced several weeks earlier than usual, in this latitude, and continued with unabated vigor for many weeks. On the 9th of January, which is just the time we generally expect the severest weather, the ice in our rivers broke up, and navigation then opened. On the 5th of February, it commenced raining, and continued to rain, with slight interruptions, until the night of the 9th instant. This rain bro't with it the snow which had accumulated during the long continuance of the cold weather. On the 9th instant [this month], our rivers commenced rising, and continued to rise regularly and rapidly until about 9 o'clock, P. M., of Friday, the 10th instant, when they were higher than had been known by any living inhabitant of this city or neighborhood.

The fresh of November, 1810, commonly called pumpkin flood, has been, heretofore, known as the highest which has occurred within the memory of any of our citizens: the recent flood exceeded it about twenty-six inches.

During the whole of Friday last, great anxiety was felt for the safety of the [Canal] Aqueduct over the Allegheny. -- The water reached the superstructure of that important work, and the immense quantity of drift, which was constantly dashing against it and accumulating so as to form a great obstruction to the flowing of the water, created a very general impression that it would be carried off. In addition to this source of anxiety, it was universally conceded, that, if the [canal] Aqueduct was destroyed, it would inevitably carry with it the valuable Bridge over the Allegheny. So general was this impression, that, we believe, an immense majority of our citizens would have cheerfully agreed to give up the Aqueduct to save the Bridge. The flood has, however, passed by the aqueduct remains uninjured: It is universally agreed that it is a perfectly sound and substantial piece of work, and Mr. Lothrop, the contractor, has the credit of performing his work faithfully.[1]

The whole of the low grounds of the boroughs of the Northern Liberties, and Allegheny, and the greater portion of that part of the City of Pittsburgh, north of Liberty street, were inundated. The damage sustained within the limits of our city was by no means equal to that sustained in those boroughs. No estimate, approaching accuracy, of the losses sustained can be made; we, therefore, for the present, decline entering into particulars."

℞

---

[1]The western division of the Main Line canal was built over the routes of the Conemaugh, Kiskiminetas and Allegheny Rivers, 1826-29. An aqueduct carried the canal across the latter at Freeport; and it continued down the west bank of the Allegheny to Allegheny City. There it connected to a "basin" and an aqueduct carried it back across the river to "downtown" Pittsburgh. The entire 395 mile route, from Philadelphia to Pittsburgh, including the 10 inclined planes and Portage Railroad over the mountains and the Philadelphia-Columbia Railroad, was completed in 1834. It was sold to the Pennsylvania RR in 1857 and soon ceased operations.

LOG RAFT DESCENDING THE ALLEGHENY RIVER, CA. 1835.
Allegheny is in the foreground. Canal aqueduct in the background.
Source: *The Story of Old Allegheny City,* (1941).

— 13 —

Pittsburgh Gazette, August 2, 1833
"SOMERSET COUNTY [& Pittsburgh's Smoke]

An intelligent friend, who has recently spent some time
in this county, gave us, yesterday, some information about
it, which may be interesting to some of our readers.

It is about 38 miles long, and 28 broad, and contains
about eleven hundred square miles. Although it extends to
the top of the Allegheny, and therefore embraces a good deal
of rough land, yet there are many pretty extensive vallies of
good arable land, and some of them well improved by thriving farmers. There is perhaps no section of the State, or
Union, more healthy and salubrious than Somerset county.

The difference of temperature, during the late warm weather, was about 12 degrees. In Somerset, the Thermometer, in the shade, ranged from 82 to 86, while at Pittsburgh the range was said to be from 92 to 96. – At Bedford the temperature is said to be about the same as at Pittsburgh. – As strong evidences of the salubrity of the climate, our friend furnished us the names of one man and his wife, who had had twenty-seven children, some of which were dead, but none died during infancy. Another, who had twenty-three children, by one wife, all living; and a third, who had twenty children – all living.

There are a variety of springs near the town of Somerset, possessed of considerable mineral properties. – For the production of potatoes, our informant states that this county is the very Ireland of America, and he also assures us that the mutton is surpassingly excellent.

A company has been incorporated to make a turnpike road from the town of Somerset to Cumberland, in Maryland. A portion of this – from Somerset to Berlin . . . [will be?] eight miles in length – will probably be completed this fall. The distance, from Berlin to Cumberland, is about twenty-two miles. This improvement is a very important one to Pittsburgh, forming as it does, a direct route of communication between this city and the National Road, at Cumberland. – When this road is completed, the distance from Cumberland to Pittsburgh (by the way of Somerset) will not exceed, by more than two or three miles, the distance from Cumberland, by the National road, to Washington, Pennsylvania. So that travelers, or merchandise, when they arrive at Cumberland, could, by the contemplated road, reach Pittsburgh by twenty-nine or thirty miles less traveling than would be required to reach Wheeling. This we consider a very important – nay, a decisive advantage, in the competition between Wheeling and Pittsburgh, for the Baltimore trade. We therefore wish that the Somerset and Cumberland Company may have both success and dispatch in completing their road.

* * * * * * *

PITTSBURGH AND HER COAL SMOKE

The opinion that the sulphur, disengaged by the consumption of stone coal, serves a valuable purpose in checking the progress of diseases among us, is by no means a new one, got up to prepare our citizens to meet, with confidence, the advance of the Asiatic Cholera. In 1826, Mr. Samuel Jones prepared a Directory of this city, and Dr. W. H. Denny furnished him a communication upon the salubrity of this place, from which we make the following abstracts, which will probably be interesting to many. What was then theory, or at last founded on a more limited experience, has, we think, been recently strongly substantiated. We believe if the Doctor had said 'there is no ague and fever,' instead of 'scarcely any,' he would have more precisely expressed the truth. It does seem, to us, that a case of ague and fever has not occurred here within the range of our recollection, which is by no means short.

Of all the great western towns, Pittsburgh is the farthest removed from the baneful exhalations of the swampy margin of the Mississippi, and accordingly enjoys a greater exemption from those diseases which, during the summer and autumn, prevail even as high up as Cincinnati. Surrounded, too, by hills and cultivated lands, and free from stagnant water, there are no local sources of disease. *The smoke of bituminous coal is anti miasmatic.* It is sulphurous and *antiseptic*, and hence it is, perhaps, that no putrid disease has ever been known to spread in the place. Strangers, with weak lungs, for a while, find their coughs aggravated by the smoke; but nevertheless, asthmatic patients have found relief in breathing it. The prevailing complaints are those which characterize the healthiest situations of the same latitude elsewhere in America – in winter, pneumonia and sore throat, and in summer, bilious affections. The goiter, or swelled neck, has disappeared; the few cases, which formerly excited the apprehensions of the stranger, no longer exist to gratify his curiosity. In comparison with the eastern cities, there is much less pulmonary consumption, less scrofula, and less disease of the skin. There is *scarcely any ague and fever*, and no yellow fever. In comparison with the western cities, including Cincinnati, there is less bilious fever; less ague and ever, and less cholera infantum, or the summer complaint of children. We are the intermediate link of disease, as well as of commerce. We have less hepatic disease than the west, and less pulmonic disease than the east.

The abundance, cheapness, and consequent general and even profuse use of the best fuel, is certainly one great cause of our superior healthfulness. The low fevers so prevalent in the large cities, among the poor, during a hard winter, and the ague so common in wet seasons, in the eastern counties of the state, where wood is scarce, are here in a great degree avoided by the universal practice of keeping good coal fires late in the spring, and early in the autumn, and indeed at all seasons when the weather is damp or inclement.

Our exemption from the ague, and epidemic dysenteries, in comparison with the settlements in the lower counties, and the eastern vallies, may be accounted for also, in part, by the scarcity of mill dams and stagnant water, in a county where in the summer, milling for the most part, is done by steam, and where the mill streams generally dry up at the season most likely to produce disease.

In the whole, with regard to the health of Pittsburgh, and indeed, of the whole western section of Pennsylvania, it may be said, that no part of the United States is more healthy, and that the greater part will bear no comparison with it in point of salubrity."[1]

Note: Preceding the "healthy smoke" comments above there is a brief piece, to wit: "CHOLERA – A boy, about eleven years of age, was taken to the Hospital, yesterday, in the last stage of collapse.- He died in a half an hour. – We have heard of no other case since we last noticed this matter."

&

— 14 —

Pittsburgh Gazette, March 15, 1837
"From *Harris' Intelligencer*, [Pittsburgh]
BUSINESS ON THE MONONGAHELA

In our youth, we often rambled along the beach, and upon the bank of the Monongahela; and at times extended our rambles to the sand-bar; opposite our city, which we have seen beautifully covered with a large crop of buck-wheat in the flower. – when a few small keel-boats were the only vehicles for the freight of the Ohio, and its tributary streams. We remember well when the 'Barge' succeeded,

---

[1]Despite the alleged "coal smoke cure" noted above, cholera came to Pittsburgh thrice in the 1830s (including 1833), once in 1849 and, again, thrice in the 1850s. During the 1854 epidemic, over 200 deaths were reported within two weeks in September!

and the arrival or departure of a large, full loaded one was a matter of great curiosity, and the town talk for days.[1] At length a few ships were built in or about Pittsburgh, and sent to sea. One was loaded and sent with a cargo to Liverpool, England; others to different parts of the world – one of which came well nigh being seized and confiscated, because the good people of a foreign land would not believe that such a place as Pittsburgh was on the face of the earth! Finally, when the immortal [Robert] Fulton built his first steamboat ('New Orleans'), [in 1811] near the present Scotch Hill Market house, on Second street, the wonder of the people was treatly excited at the great improvement of the times. Gradually Steamboat business has been brought to great perfection, and almost ceases to be a matter of interest with the mass. So great is the improvement in our freighting and carrying trade; and such an immense business is now doing on the Monongahela wharf, and along the river, that we resolved to spend a leisure hour on Thursday afternoon [March 9], in taking a 'Business view of matters and things.' With pencil and book in hand, we commenced our tour at Messrs. Bakewell and Co.'s excellent wharf, at the foot of Grant street, where the view of the business above the Bridge is excellent: thence to our friend Hart's, at the Monongahela bridge where we had an extended prospect, up and down, and thence deliberately to Wood, Market, Ferry and Liberty streets, to the Point and the site of old Fort Duquesne. The whole shore of the river was covered with boats, receiving and delivering goods. Bales of cotton, boxes, barrels, pack-

---

[1]Barges were much wider and usually the same length as keelboats, with a draft of 3-4 feet. They had masts and sails, for the lower rivers, and were steered by a rudder. They were rowed and poled upstream with crews carrying ca. 40 tons of freight, until later years when they were longer and could carry over 175 tons.

ages, dray, and merchandise of all kinds, covered the beach until we reached Ferry street, where a long string of large and excellent <u>new steamboats</u> are moored, in different stages of finish, all of which will be ready in a a few days or weeks to take in cargoes and depart for all parts of the rivers below. We counted the following number of boats from Suke's run to the Point, viz: of steamboats now in port, 28 – and 7 that departed this day, making 35 steamboats, 30 keels, and 23 arks, or large flat boats; making in all 88 boats. We intended to have given a list of the size, tonnage, name, captain and destination of each boat; but as we could not procure a correct one in time, we were obliged to omit it.[2]

On our return home we met a friend who is engaged largely in the Commission and Steamboat business, who remarked, that he believed we had sent off within a few days so many steamboats, that we had on this day fewer to port than is common for this season of the year."

༄

---

[2]This is an important observation concerning the overall commercial activity on the Mon. The writer is correct; river news and steamboat activity had become, by 1837, rather mundane. For example, on the same day, March 9, the *Pittsburgh Gazette* reported only 3 steamboat arrivals and 3 departures. On April 15, just 3 departures were reported.

15

Harris' Intelligencer (Pittsburgh), June 22, 1839
"THE CITY OF ALLEGHENY –
DELIGHTFUL SCENERY –
FUTURE GREATNESS

We this week, spent a very pleasant afternoon upon the delightful hills around this new and beautiful city. We first ascended the height at knobs on Nunnery Hill, which we found in a good state of cultivation, and from which you have very expansive and beautiful views of both cities, the three rivers, and immense improvements and business population around and before you; the delightful hills and dales along the Allegheny [River] on both sides, and of those distant and beautiful full tops, back and to the North, East, and South, and many handsome country seats, gardens, villages, &c. as far as the eye can reach, eastward. We then turned and crossed the field, passed the coal pits, near Montgomery's house, and then verged towards the city again, and took a fresh stand and survey from the top of another beautiful hill, where in our juvenile days, an old man lived and supported a large family, by raising Water and Musk melons, and an immense quantity of pumpkins, which gave the name to this elevated spot of 'Pumpkin hill,' by which we believe it has ever since been known. Here again you have new and beautiful views of Allegheny, Pittsburgh, and almost all the towns and villages, bridges, canal, and public buildings, &c. Here you can meditate in silence, and view a large part of the surrounding scenery, and you are here just back of the Western Penitentiary, where more than a hundred unfortunate inmates are labouring to atone to society for crimes against the public peace. And here too you can view the little space of four or five miles around Pittsburgh, in which is about 60,000 inhabitants, upwards of fifty Churches, and as many Sabbath Schools, two Theological Seminaries, several male and female Seminaries, &c.&c. in which upwards of thirty millions of dollars in business is annually transacted, with a sure and steady increase, and which in twenty-five years more will contain near a quarter of a million of inhabitants, with a corresponding increase in business, moral, religious, and literary advances. Here too on these beautiful heights nature is rich and prolific. As we turned to pursue our journey, we were pleased with the richness of the soil, the land covered with clover and fine grass, and droves of cattle enjoying themselves on the [?] of the land. We then passed through a grove of woods to a private road (owned and used by Germans and others who keep dairies and follow gardening) and made a circuit, coming into the rear of Mr. Swaney's new and beautiful establishment, on top of the hill immediately over the western part of Allegheny and Manchester. Here we were agreeably surprised and delighted – not with the new and beautiful views, and expansive and delightful scenery – but with the very judicious location, the vast and very appropriate improvements, made upon it in a single year. Mr. Swaney has built and finished a handsome house, surrounded on all sides with porches, and upon the top an Arena for the purpose of viewing the beautiful [h]eights, landscapes, country seats, gardens, and around it – in every direction and to a great distance. Here you have at once new and beautiful scenes of Allegheny and Pittsburgh, the [canal] aqueduct and three bridges, and most of the public improvements in and around both cities. Just below you lies the lovely cluster of lots and ground from the Penitentiary to Manchester, which affords room for an immense city, and the many new and beautiful country seats of our rich and enterprising citizens, now covering a part of it, will in less than 25 years in all human probability, give way to city improvements and possibly an active population of near 100,000 souls. Here too you have a beautiful view of the three rivers – the Allegheny and Monongahela meeting at the point and forming the beautiful Ohio, which is just below you, and you can here see every steam boat arriving and departing, and with a telescope can read their names, and discriminate the passengers on board. You have also here a beautiful view of the lovely scenery on the hills over the Monongahela river. Temperance village, Bailey's springs, Adam's beautiful Island, mouth of Chartiers creek, and McKees Rock behind it, and a vast variety of beautiful scenery, which we for want of room to describe recommend all to go and see and view for themselves.

We then made a hasty visit to the new and pretty village of Manchester, and on returning homeward, we had just time to pass over Seminary Hill, a very desirable spot from whence you have at once many new and beautiful views of both cities, the rivers and surrounding scenery. On the hill the Presbyterians have erected a large and spacious seminary for the education, boarding, &c. of candidates for the Ministry. There is now upwards of 30 students in it. From this institution the hill derives its name. After a most pleasing and interesting walk around our new and beautiful city of Allegheny, we returned home just in time to partake of a hearty supper, for which our travels on the hill gave us a double zest."[1]

---

[1]Allegheny became a 3rd class "city" in 1840 with a population of 10,090. (Pittsburgh had 21,000). By 1891, it had become a 2nd class city and by 1900 had a population of 129,000. Talk of being annexed by Pittsburgh began in 1846. Annexation legislation was defeated in 1853-54 and 1873. In 1898, the annexationists got the legislature to approve a vote by both cities. Pittsburgh won

16

Monongahela Republican, October 26, 1840
"Correspondence of the Cleveland Herald
October, 1840

Friend Harris – Would that I had the pen of the 'Wizzard of the North,' to describe to you the Birmingham of America. But it is impossible for me to picture to 'the mind's eye' the rich and varied scenery around this city. The beauty of its location is unequalled. Whichever way you turn, you behold gently sloping hills rising on either side, dotted with splendid country seats, and elegant cottages, the abode of virtue, intelligence and warm hearted hospitality. 'Coal Hill' is somewhat *right up and down*, as a Yankee would say. It lies so that both sides of it can be filled. Its coal beds are as inexhaustible as the particles of light; and for succeeding ages will be a source of wealth to the owners.

As this is my first visit to the city of manufactures and of smoke, I am very much 'happily' disappointed in its appearance. I supposed from what I had heard about this place, that a man could hardly find his way through the streets at noon-day, without a light. True, the city has rather a *dusky* hue; but in clear weather, this is a pleasant, place. It has not, to be sure, the white and snowy appearance of our 'City of the Lakes,' but then, the streets are clean and neat; and on Saturday afternoon the whole city is

---

handily; but the vote was appealed to the U. S. Supreme court. It declared the legislative act unconstitutional. In 1906, another bill was passed, another election occurred and it was, again, appealed. The Supreme Court approved the entire process and the merger became effective on Dec. 9, 1907.

scrubbed; and good luck to him who passes along the streets without getting wet.

The streets here are narrow, with the exception of Liberty and Penn, perhaps, and they run *every which way.* One might about as well endeavor to get out of a *Labyrinth,* as to find his way to any particular place in this city. I could only find both ends. It takes a stranger, especially if he has not the *bump of locality* fully developed, some time to get the *hang* of Pittsburgh.

Work shops, houses, manufacturing establishments, private residences, bakeries, rolling mills, &c., &. [?] are mixed up here in glorious confusion. Adjoining an elegant private residence, you will see an Iron establishment. At one glance you will see furnace-men covered with sweat and coal dust, and at the next you will behold a fair young being, with cheeks 'rosy as the morn,' at the window plying the needle of industry.

At the right you will hear the rattling noise of machinery, the sound of the hammer, and the implements of industry; and on the left you will hear the music of the piano, and a sweet voice, gushing out in the full rich melody of song, 'For Tippecanoe and Tyler too.'[1]

It is strange that the people here are not all deaf, for really this is a noisy city, for these workers in Iron and Brass can no more be quiet, than the Whigs can *about these days.*

This is a place of business, and every body is busy. I do not believe that there is an idle man, woman or child, in

---

[1]This was the first political slogan in a U.S. presidential election. "Tippecanoe" referred to William Henry Harrison, the Whig presidential candidate in 1840, who was the "hero" of the defeat of Native Americans in the village of Tippecanoe in present-day Indiana in 1811. John Tyler was the vice-presidential candidate from Virginia.

this city. A *drone* cannot live in such a place as this. His locomotives would be set in motion unconsciously to himself. He would work, because he could not help it – There would be a kind of an instinctive do-something-for-a-living in him. He would labor out of mere sympathy.

The streets are constantly filled with drays laden with 'goods, wares and merchandize,' and an abundance of domestic manufactures. A very heavy wholesale business is done here in goods and groceries. All kinds of trade seems to be as flourishing as the pecuniar[y] state of the country will at present admit.

The population of Pittsburgh and Allegheny cities, and the villages in the vicinity, including a circuit of five miles square, is estimated at 60,000. The home manufactures and mechanical production amount to $12,000,000 annually. There are 60 places of religious worship. Pittsburgh has ever been celebrated for its high moral and religious character. I noticed here on the Sabbath, that the streets were filled with church going people. The man who will not shave and put on a clean shirt on the Sabbath, is not a good member of society. Trust not such a man. He will do any dirty work. Here are a 100 schools of various kinds – many of them 'public schools' where the children of all are educated at the expense of the public, as they should be. Every dollar, tax, that a man pays for the purposes of education, is only a small premium, as additional security on his property, his life and his liberty.

Here are 9 Banks and Insurance companies, employing a capital of $5,000,000. Twenty newspapers, truly this speaks well. They must be here a reading, as they are a highly intelligent people. Daily lines of stage coaches and canal boats, 20: — single and double lines of canal freight boats, 11: — annual arrivals and departures of steam vessels engaged in the river trade, 2,500: — annual sales in the various departments of merchandize, $13,000,000: — annual amount of freight or merchandize and produce passing through the account of non-resident owners, $3,000,000. – This last item will be greatly increased in consequence of the construction of the canal from Beaver to Akron; and this new channel of communication, will open a vast country for Pittsburgh to supply with her manufactures. So much for the home industry and business of this western Birmingham.

Fifty years ago, Pittsburgh was 'a little inland isle, . . . by a forest sea embraced;' and here and there only did the smoke of the 'cabin' of the white man, ascend west of the frowning and cloud covered Alleghanies. What a change in half a century! It is unequalled, and unparalleled in the history of the world! Fifty years ago, the sly fox, the growling bear, and the timid deer, wandered undisturbed, o'er the now beautiful and cultivated hills and valleys in the vicinity of this flourishing place. The evening fires of the Indian curled up amid the branches of the forest trees – and the waters of the Allegheny, the Monongahela and the *La Belle Riviere*, [the French term for the Ohio River] rolled silently from the mountains to the ocean, save when they echoed the boat song of the Indian, or the battle shout of savage warfare. What a change! The forests have been felled by the 'woodman's axes' – the wilderness has disappeared – and in the place of gloomy wilds, are cultivated farms and smiling fields and elegant farm houses, the abode of industry and virtue, and knowledge.

Upon the waters, in the place of the red man's canoe, that danced over their surface like an airy thing, is the noble steam boat, dashing along 'like a thing of life,' having in tow less comely craft, freighted with the productions of the workshop, and of the fertile earth. How much are we indebted to the genius of a [Robert] Fulton! And yet his family live in poverty [in Washington Co.]. Oh! Shame, my countrymen!

82

Thousands to foreign dancers or hoppers, but not a farthing to the family of him who annihilated space by the use of steam.

The new Court House, when finished, will be one of the most splendid and magnificent buildings in the Union. Its location is commanding on 'Grant's Hill.' And this hill should have been preserved. From the rotunda of the Court House, is one of the most beautiful views in our country. Cities and villages, with their 'busy hum' of industry, and pleasant farms, under a high state of cultivation, are before you. Private residences, of rich and truly hospital [hospitable?] citizens are scattered along on the banks of the winding rivers, in every direction; and these are as beautiful, as elegant, as finely decorated with trees, and shurbs, and flowering plants, and as well adorned by the hand of culti-vated taste, as man can wish for. But, I fear the material of which the Court House is made, will not stand the *destroying tooth of time.* It is a sandstone, and the sulphide of iron mixed with it, will cause the stone to crumble or peal off. But this may not be so.

Society here is most excellent. The people are frank, hospitable, generous, intelligent and high minded. Here peo-ple live to enjoy life. Parties here, are exceedingly pleasant and social. I hardly dare trust myself to speak of the *'better half'* of our race—

'For even from my boyhood's hour, my mind
Has been a willing slave, to woman's witchery:'

But this much I dare say, that if any one wishes to find ladies more lovely and accomplished than the Ladies of Pitts-burgh and Allegheny, I do not know where he will go to find them.

I have written you a long all sorts of a letter, and have written not a word about many things and places I desire to.

If any one has leisure, and wishes to pass a week pleasantly, let him visit Pittsburgh."

PITTSBURGH AND ALLEGHENY, 1849.
Source: *Fleming's Views of Old Pittsburgh.*

— 17 —

Pittsburgh Daily Gazette, July 31, 1849
"TRIP TO THE COUNTRY NO. 1

We determined last week to breathe, for a few hours at least, the pure air of the country, so leaving Pittsburgh, we rode via Birmingham and Street's Run, to West Elizabeth. The ride was a very pleasant one, since we passed through a section of country as much favored by nature, in regard to beautiful scenery, as any other with which we are acquainted.

We saw, on all sides, numerous indications of the prosperity of that most estimable class of our citizens, the farmers, in the shape of well filled barns – neat dwelling houses – fine orchards – well tilled and fertile field, and stock of the very best descriptions. West Elizabeth is a pretty little town, inhabited by a thriving population, whose chief business is coal boating. The bill of one firm alone, which ships coal [on barges] to New Orleans, was $1000 in six months, for stores furnished to the crews of their boats. The business like town of Elizabeth is opposite to this place, and is particularly noted for the excellence of the steam boats built in its boat yards. The branch of business, which has been rather dull for some time past, is now rapidly reviving, and will, we hope, be shortly as flourishing as ever. Three or four very fine boats, are now on hand in various yards. The flouring mill of the Messrs. Applegate is doing a good business, and the numerous saw mills around seem to prosper. The Mansion House kept by Mr. James Milliki, is an excellent hotel, and one which we can conscientiously, judging from personal experience, recommend to our friends. The Exchange Hotel, Mr. D. Sarver, Proprietor, is also deserving the attention of travelers, since its landlord is a very worthy and polite gentleman.

A pleasant ride brought us to Monongahela City six miles from Elizabeth. This town is a very thriving one, -- well built, and rapidly growing [as?] an important place. The numerous glass works, foundries, flour, and saw mills, tan yards, and the fine woolen manufactory now in process of creation, all indicate that it is inhabited by an industrious population.

The country, all around, is a very fertile one and we should say, from examination, that the yield of oats and hay has been very heavy this year, though the wheat crop has been somewhat injured by the rust. We were delighted with our ride from Monongahela City to Brownsville, though we missed the way, and spent some time longer on the road than we would have done were it not for this accident. The sun was setting, as we approached it, and we could see his rays reflected from the windows of some houses about 15 miles distant, gleaming like burnished gold. The dark masses of foliage crowning their sides agreeably relieved by the golden hue of the crops on the cleared portions, together made a scene of beauty well worthy the pencil of the painter.

The busy town of Brownsville, with its noise and smoke, always appears to us like a miniature Pittsburgh. The buildings of which the town is composed, are very much scattered, though fast filling up, and assuming that SOLIDARITY of appearance so indicative of a thriving business town.

The daily line of steam boats between Brownsville and the place bring them within a few hours travel of each other and the morning papers of Pittsburgh are sold in Brownsville in the afternoon.[1] We were glad to see in most of the farm houses on our route that the *Gazette* was taken and properly appreciated. It has a large circulation in this region.

We will to morrow give a description of our visit to Uniontown and Fayette Springs."

$\mathcal{R}$

---

[1]The writer does not indicate that the Monongahela Navigation Company had built 4 locks and dams on the Mon by 1844, with a six-foot channel from Pittsburgh to Brownsville, opening regular navigation for the first time. The Pittsburgh and Brownsville Packet Company ran three steamboats daily on the 56-mile trade. The *Atlantic* and *Baltic* (188 tons each) were built in Brownsville in

Pittsburgh Daily Gazette, August 2, 1849
"TRIP TO THE COUNTRY, NO. 2

The National Road from Brownsville to Uniontown is kept in very good order, and passes through a fine, fertile country. Uniontown is a charming little place, and the great number of stages which pass through it every day relieves it from that monotony so unpleasant in most country towns.

It is delightfully situated in a valley surrounded by hills, and is almost twelve miles from the Monongahela and eleven from the Youghiogheny. -- The Court House of Fayette County is a neat, unpretending structure of brick, (we are sorry that we cannot say much for the gaol [jail]-, and there is a very good alms house just outside the town, Uniontown, likewise, contains several churches, manufactories, and hotels, one of which kept by Mr. A. Stone, is very worthy the attention of travelers.

A rapid ride [north] of about fifteen miles brought us to Perryopolis, a pleasant little town, rapidly increasing in importance. It contains the glass works of Messrs. Herron and Welges [?], together with saw mills, tan yards, and other indications of business. This town is interesting in another particular, since the country for several miles around it, formerly belongs to General Washington, who had a house built here, when all around was a forest, and is said to have superintended the erection of one of the saw mills. The

---

1848. They ran on the Mon until dismantled in 1856 and 1854, respectively. The 175-ton *Louis McLane*, was built in Brownsville in 1845. She was named for the president of the B&O Railroad, probably because the line had been built to Cumberland, Md., where one could take a stage to Brownsville, then connecting downriver by steamer. She ran on the Mon until being dismantled in 1850.

name of this great and good man has been given to several resorts in this vicinity.

Before returning home, we paid a short visit to Fayette Springs, about eight miles [east] from Uniontown, and found it crowded with visitors, about eighty of whom were Pittsburghers, who appeared to spend their time very pleasantly. [See No. 23.]

The manufacture of window glass, in particular, is carried on in the valley of the Monongahela to an extent of which few of our readers have any idea, and is a source of wealth both to the manufacturer, and the surrounding farmers. We may take, as one out of many, the establishment of Mr. R. Smith of Elizabeth, which turns out about seven thousand boxes of glass, worth four dollars per box, every ten months. The country along the Monongahela, taken as a whole, is one of the most beautiful and fertile valleys in Pennsylvania inhabited by an honest, energetic, and wealthy population."

∽

— 19 —

Pittsburgh Daily Gazette, December 9, 1851
"THE FIRST RAILROAD TRAIN FROM
PENNSYLVANIA TO OHIO

On yesterday we had the satisfaction of passing into Ohio, from Pennsylvania, in the first railroad train which ever passed from Keystone into the Buckeye State. This, to the superficial observer, may seem but a trivial event, but it will be viewed differently by discriminating and reflecting minds. Thirty-three years ago, this month, we first passed the dividing line between Pennsylvania and Ohio, on a shocking road, from which the stumps of the original forest trees were not cleared, and when the greatest part of that now magnificent State was a vast wilderness. Yesterday, within a few miles of the same spot, we passed the line by railroad, -- that great modern agent of civilization and commerce, -- with the accompaniments of the roaring of artillery, the whistling of the locomotive, and the glad shouts of the inhabitants. These great States, with a homogeneous population, and identity of interests, and holding a control, and we may say a controlling influence in binding and cementing this glorious Union, and now united together literally by bars of iron, . . .

At 8 o'clock, yesterday morning, we took our seat in the express train of the Ohio and Pennsylvania Railroad, bound on its first voyage to Ohio. At 10 minutes past 10 we arrived at Enon and leaving the mails and passengers for New Castle, Poland, and Warren, we started for Palestine, [Oh.] and at 26 minutes past 10 afterwards, arrived at Palestine, 40 miles from Pittsburgh. This little village had poured forth all its population to do honor to this important event in its history. A cannon was posted on an acclivity, which was served with skill and celerity from the moment we passed the State line, until we landed amidst the cheers and congratulations of the citizens.

We spent several hours here very pleasantly. A magnificent dinner was provided at the private residence of Dr. Chamberlain, one of the principal proprietors of the place, to which a number of gentlemen, officers of the road and invited guests, did ample justice. Dr. Chamberlain, Mr. Brewster, and other citizens vied with each other in giving the Pennsylvanians a hearty welcome into Ohio.

Palestine is very pleasantly situated in the valley of the Little Beaver [River], in the midst of a fine agricultural country, with abundance of excellent coal, and near good mills. The road runs through the place on a level with the ground, affording great facilities for building, with little or no expense for grading. We expect to see a thriving and active place spring up here. What is now wanted especially is a good hotel of respectable dimensions. We understand that Dr. Chamberlain is willing to give the necessary ground to any persons who will put up such a house, which we have no doubt would do well. A great deal of freight must be loaded at this point, and we learned that large quantities of produce are now waiting the arrival of the freight train. Messrs. Boyd and Mardock, of Allegheny, are putting up buildings along the line with a celerity almost unprecedented.

At 20 past two o'clock, P.M., we left on our return, and started to the inspiriting roar of the cannon. The fine piece of artillery was the same used on the 4th of July, 1849, when the celebration of breaking ground at the State line took place. A little over two years have passed, and notwithstanding some croakers on that day sagely predicted the road would never be built, the same cannon has already signalized the opening of the road to the same point and beyond it. This is loud and just testimony to the energy of those gentlemen who had it in charge.

We arrived safe home at five o'clock, much gratified with our excursion in the first Railroad train which ever passed from Pennsylvania to Ohio."[1]

---

[1]The railroad, the first in the Pittsburgh area, had been completed to New Brighton on July 30, 1851. It soon connected with the Cleveland and Cincinnati Railroad, making a line between Pittsburgh and Cleveland. It continued, as the Pittsburgh, Ft. Wayne and Chicago Railroad, to push northwest through Ohio and into Indiana toward Chicago.

20

Pittsburgh Gazette, December 11, 1851
"OPENING OF THE PENNSYLVANIA RAILROAD

The opening of the Pennsylvania [Central] Railroad, from Pittsburgh to Turtle Creek, took place yesterday, and was signaled by an excursion trip given on the part of the Company to a number of gentlemen, comprehending the Mayor and Councils of the two cities, stockholders, public officers, editorial corps, etc. The cars left the station on Liberty Street, just above the Canal Bridge, at a quarter past eleven, and arrived at the Turtle Creek station at 12, P.M. It was snowing hard at the time, and the track was not, therefore, in a situation for high speed, even were such desirable in a first trip. The road is a first rate one, the superstructure being very solid, and the cars running very quietly. The Cars are of the first class, and the handsomest, taken as a whole, we have ever seen. They are truly luxurious. At Wilkinsburgh and at Turtle Creek very handsome station houses have been erected, and at the latter place there is a turntable, to answer the purposes of an accommodation train to that point.

A large hotel has been erected at the Turtle Creek station, which is kept by Mr. Shepherd, and although he has only been in it about a week, he furnished for the guests, on behalf of the Railroad Company, an excellent dinner, to which ample justice was done.

. . . At the conclusion of the meeting, the company re-entered the cars, and in about forty minutes arrived in the city, every person expressing satisfaction with the trip.

To-day the regular line to Philadelphia is open . . . ."[1]

෫

---

[1] The railroad, which included the Columbia and Portage Railroads, was not completed from Philadelphia until Nov. 29, 1852. With the completion of the mountain division two years later, the Pennsylvania Central's trains were able to traverse the 300-mile unified route. Three trains ran daily, making the 300-mile trek in 13-17 hours.

This represented a major victory for Philadelphia's efforts to reach the Ohio prior to the Baltimore and Ohio RR. It had a charter to build to Wheeling via Brownsville, Pa. It got to Cumberland, Md., in 1842; but the Virginia legislature delayed in extending it to the Panhandle. Pittsburgh wanted it instead and lobbied the legislature for a B&O bill. Philadelphia, however, was able to ram through a Pennsylvania Central Railroad Bill and a B&O Bill in April, 1846. But the latter included a proviso that if the former could raise $4 million and build 30 miles of track by July 30, 1847, the B&O charter would be voided. It seemed impossible, but it did and it was! The B&O was forced to build west to Wheeling via Grafton, Va. The route opened in Jan. 1853.

WELCOMING COMMITTEE   On December 10, 1852, a crowd gathered at East Liberty to welcome the first through-train from the east. Source: Stefan Lorant, *Pittsburgh: The Story of an American City* (Lenox, MA: R. R. Donnelley & Sons, 1975).

21

Pittsburgh Gazette, April 20, 1852
"GREAT FLOOD

For more than three days rain has fallen almost incessantly, and much of the time heavily, and as a consequence, all the streams are in high flood. The rivers here, which for some days had been receding from the high freshet of week before last, commenced rising rapidly on Sunday morning, and up to 10 o'clock that night had attained to the alarming height of 23 feet above low water mark.

During that day many rafts were driven by the force of the current from their moorings along the shores of the Allegheny, and carried down the stream. Some of these rafts were broken against the piers of the bridges, and it is reported that two or three lives were lost; but we are unable to trace the rumors to any authentic source.

Monday – During all Sunday night, and up to 8 P. M. on Monday, the hour at which we write, the rain continued to pour down in torrents, and the rivers to advance steadily at the rate of seven to eight inches per hour, when it had reached the great height of 80 to 81 feet above low water. All the low ground in this city, from the Point to the extremity of the 8th ward, along the Allegheny, is overflowed. All the short streets running from Penn street to the Allegheny are more or less covered with water. The City Water Works, and all the rolling mills and foundries on Etna Street are surrounded and drowned out. Innumerable cellars are filled, and the water is on the first floors of many dwellings.

But this city is not suffering so severely as our sister city, Allegheny. All that part of that city below the canal and along the river, is covered with water to a considerable depth. Even Federal street, between the river and canal, and all that portion of the city above Federal street, for about three squares back from the river, are also flooded, but to a less depth.

The losses sustained already in lumber, and in the damage to buildings and other property, is very considerable. Many families have been obliged to leave their dwellings and seek shelter among their more elevated neighbors.

Both our rivers are in full flood, and both yet rising rapidly. Neither affects perceptibly the current of the other. Both are covered with drift wood. The appearance of the Allegheny, rushing along, as it is bounded by the houses of the two cities, is truly grand.

Redbank creek, a tributary of the Allegheny, was very high on Sunday, and causes great destruction of property, particularly lumber, near all of which was swept out. We have not heard from the Kiskiminietas, but were informed yesterday that a hill slide filled the canal below Freeport. It is said that it can be cleared out again in a day or two.

4 o'clock – The water has now reached to within four feet of the height of the great flood of 1832, and is rising at the rate of four inches an hour. It is still raining slightly.

The turnpike bridge at Turtle creek was carried away this afternoon by the back water from the Monongahela. This is a serious affair, as it will interrupt for a time the travel by the [Pennsylvania] Central Railroad. It was reported that the bridge over the Monongahela at Brownsville was carried away, but we hope it is not true. Up to this hour we have no dispatches from that place.

The water is over the Ohio and Pennsylvania Railroad in several places between this and New Brighton. No trains can pass either way until the flood subsides.

The cellars along Water street and the lower end of Wood street have been cleared of their contents, and some of them are beginning to fill with water. The ground on that side of the city is higher than on the Allegheny side.

6 o'clock -- Still raining, and the water rising rapidly. This will be a terrible night in Allegheny. The water is to the second stories in many houses. There is much distress. The unabated rise has induced many families to abandon their dwellings before night, and men are to be seen in all quarters wading through the streets carrying their children to places of safety, there not being enough of boats to accommodate all.

The *Chronicle* states, on the authority of a passenger by the railroad, that the Conemaugh is higher than ever it was before known to be. It is to be feared that the canal will be extensively injured. A gentleman who has just come down the Allegheny states that the amount of water to come down is without precedent.

The Allegheny *Enterprise* of yesterday afternoon gives the following picture of the state of things in that city at noon yesterday:

In this city, the water has covered a large portion of the 1st and 4th Wards. The residents in the lowest part of the 4th Ward made arrangements yesterday to remove to the upper part of the city. The continued advance of the water has caused great confusion in some streets considered 'high and dry.' This morning we notice the demand for skifts [skiffs?], furniture wagons, drays, &c., on the increase – the water reaching some parts of the city heretofore considered secure against high water. – Today, at 10 o'clock, A. M., the water was overflowing Robinson st., Sandusky st., Craig st., Bank Lane, and Lacock st. The water in the Allegheny has backed up the Pennsylvania canal to the height of 6 feet – rendering the tow path impassable, and covering all the lots between Federal, Sandusky, and Lacock streets. On the lower side of Federal street, towards the junction of the rivers, the entire bottom is overflowed – in some places the water reaching to the second story of the dwelling house.

That paper gives the following table of the rise each hour, from noon on Sunday till noon on Monday:

Stages of Water – We are indebted to the gentlemanly clerks at the toll house of the Aqueduct, for the following table of the rates which the Allegheny River has risen each hour, from 12 o'clock, M., yesterday (Sunday) up to 12 o'clock, M., today:

From 12 up to 1	it rose	6¾ inches
From 1 to 2	it rose	7¾ inches
From 2 to 3	it rose	8½ inches
From 3 to 4	it rose	8¾ inches
From 4 to 5	it rose	7 inches
From 5 to 6	it rose	8 inches
From 6 to 7	it rose	8 inches
From 7 to 8	it rose	7½ inches
From 8 to 9	it rose	8 inches
From 9 to 10	it rose	4¾ inches
From 10 to 11	it rose	6½ inches
From 11 to 12	it rose	6½ inches
From 12 to 1	it rose	6¾ inches
From 1 to 2	it rose	6¼ inches
From 2 to 3	it rose	6 inches
From 3 to 4	it rose	6½ inches
From 4 to 5	it rose	6½ inches
From 5 to 6	it rose	6½ inches
From 6 to 7	it rose	6½ inches
From 7 to 8	it rose	6½ inches
From 8 to 9	it rose	4½ inches
From 9 to 10	it rose	4½ inches
From 10 to 11	it rose	5 inches
From 11 to 12	it rose	4¼ inches

Total rise in last 24 hours – 155 inches."

22

Pittsburgh Daily Gazette, September 14, 1855
"OPENING OF THE PITTSBURGH AND
CONNELLSVILLE RAILROAD.

Half an hour after midnight, on Wednesday night, or rather Thursday morning, the 'excursionists' stepped from the steamer *Eolian*[1] upon the well-known cobble-stones of the Monongahela Wharf, and there was thereafter immediately many hurrings homeward – many patterings of weary feet on the pavements. As we passed by our office, the sound of the mallet pounding these columns into condition of fixity, warned us that the compositor had laid by his 'stick and rule,' and we were saved the weary labor of preparing a report of the 'opening' while all the rest of men were dozing away the quiet and 'we sma' hours 'ayant the twal.' With that, we wended our weary way homeward, and 'the thunders did roll and the lightnings did rattle' and the clouds came down bodily, and we received a precious good ducking. With the rain came a cold, and that uncomfortable malady chose our head as the particular portion of our system in which to take up its abode. Of all things despicable, awful, infernal, a 'cold in the head' is the despicablest, awfullest, infernallest, and to that our readers must attribute any short-comings in this our brief report of the great 'opening.'

Having chronicled the precise hour at which the *Eolian* returned, we may remark that she left this city on Tuesday

---

[1]The 178-ton *Eolian* was built in Brownsville in 1855. It ran on the Mon and made trips up the Youghiogheny. In 1857-59, it was a packet on the Minnesota River and was off the steamboat lists in 1853.

afternoon, at 4 o'clock, having on board about one hundred Pittsburghers and Alleghenians, including members of the Councils, officers of the Road, the Reporters (ubiquitous rascals!), a goodly sprinkling of the legal profession, and, finally, Capt. Pratt.

The trip up the [Monongahela] river was unattended by any incident worthy of record. We have heretofore described the scenery of the 'Yock' [Youghiogheny River] and given some idea of the vastness of the coal and mineral deposits along its banks. It is truly a wonderful region, teeming with the natural wealth and those natural advantages which give stability to empires. But the shades of evening had crept upon us ere we passed McKeesport, and our company were compelled to exercise their ingenuity in inventing means of amusement. The whist-table found numerous votaries, and had rivals in the attractions of others games. Everybody, not engaged in making 'points' or 'books,' or 'going five better,' were doing up the conversational in fine style. Some, but very few, were poking old Bacchus in the ribs, while others were getting tan in the noisy mazes of the stag-dance. But twilight came and all was still, save the measured 'puff! puff!' of the engine and long, nocturnal[?] snore of some sleeper. Those who were unfortunate as not to have obtained state-rooms, tried the virtues of the floor, and when morning came we awoke in West Newton.

At half past eight, a train conveying at least one thousand persons left West Newton for Connellsville, drawn by two locomotives. In something more than an hour, Connellsville – the mecca of our pilgrimage – burst upon our vision. And a very pretty town it is. Like West Newton, it is pitched upon a hill side leading to the river, and of necessity its principal streets are not of very comfortable ascent. Opposite Connellsville is the small ville of New Haven, which contains a very large Wool and Cotton factory. Connellsville itself has about thirteen hundred inhabitants. It is increasing. The rail road, which is the great Civilizer, has inspired it with new life. It is waking up to some hopes of a return of that prosperity which it enjoyed of old, for Connellsville is no mushroom settlement, but is venerable with the snows of fifty years. It was a great depot of Emigration in the early times, and here too, the manufacture of cannon balls and other munitions of war was carried on extensively during the war of 1812. Property has recently taken a long leap on a highly gratifying manner. But we are forgetting the train.

As the engine flew, screaming, into the town, a piece of ordnance belched forth a thunderous welcome, and enveloped the multitude in a thick cloud of white smoke. When the cannon had done firing, the infantry (five companies) ranged on the hill above the track, fired a salute. Then the bands struck up, and the multitude cheered and threw up hats. It was quite an animated scene. The military immediately formed in columns and marched. We were so busily engaged in watching something grotesque that one or two of the 'sogers' that we missed the speeches.

Upon inquiry we found that the Hon. Andrew Stewart, of Uniontown, had addressed a response to the welcome of Connellsville, and was followed on the party of Allegheny county with a few appropriate remarks by James S. Craft, Esq., President of the Steubenville road. These proceedings through, the crowd moved, sprinkling itself in spots about the town, and many repairing to the Railroad Grove, about three-quarters of a mile west of the town, where the Free Celebration Dinner was to take place.

We went back to the military. There was an encampment in the village, and thither the soldiers marched. The tents, which were twenty-three in number, were pitched on the side of a hill – not in very beautiful order, nor in a position at all captivating.

The encampment was commanded by Major George White, Brigade inspector, assisted by Major I.A. Moreland and Col. R.H. Austin. The following companies were present:

Union Volunteers, of Uniontown, Capt, King.

Green Mountain Blues, of East Liberty, Fayette County, Capt. Brown.

Flat Woods Guards, of Flat Woods, Fayette County, Capt. Abrams.

Falls City Guard, of Falls City [Ohiopyle], Captain Jackson.

Youghiogheny Blues, of Connellsville, Capt. Walker.

Union Artillery, of Uniontown, Capt. Patrick.

The whole number of men in camp is about one hundred and sixty. The camp began on Tuesday and was concluded yesterday. We cannot say very much about the military skill of the men in camp, except the Artillery whose displays were creditable. There was scarcely a sign of discipline, and the marching was decidedly 'awkward squak-ish.' We were however informed by one of the officers that many of the men were substitutes, unused to handling arms.

At 12 o'clock, a procession was formed, headed by the military, and a numerous crowd marched to the Grove, where dinner was prepared. Five tables, each at least one hundred and fifty yards long, had been ranged in parallels, and were groaning beneath a profusion of eatables! When the siege began, the multitude were appreciative of the excellence of the viands [dishes of food]. The provisions were good, but there was no provision for eating them, except 'these five pokers and etealers.[?]' Not a plate, knife or fork was to be seen, which was bad – very bad.

Stomachs being full, the assemblage was organized by calling Judge GILLMORE, of Uniontown, to the Chair. Addresses were delivered by the following gentlemen: — Judge Gillmore, Alfred Paterson, Esq., Gen. Joshua D. Howell, -?.B.

Miller, Esq., and Amzi Fuller, Esq., all of Uniontown. We deem it unnecessary to present any report of their remarks. The general tenor of their speeches was the propriety of an immediate subscription of $250,000 by Fayette county to the capital stock of the Road. There was considerable enthusiasm manifested, and we have no doubt the moral effect of this vast convention of the people will result in the subscription mentioned, which, with a helping hand from our sister city, Allegheny, and a big push from Baltimore, will soon send the locomotive speeding through from Pittsburgh to Cumberland [Md.]. 'A consummation most devoutly to be wished.'

The exercises at the Grove concluded, we returned to the town, where our delegates whiled away the afternoon until the arrival of the cars at half past three. Some difficulty occurred here on account of the crowding. Probably one half of the multitude had never before that day seen a locomotive and their highest ambition was to get a ride in the cars. This determination was carried out somewhat to the violation of the rules of courtesy, but we finally got under way, and were speeding briskly away over the well-land (laid) track toward West Newton, where we arrived at half past four. In half an hour, the *Elion's* bow was pointing homeward and a very good supper was vanishing fast away.

About nine o'clock a meeting was called to give expression of the feelings of the excursionists of Pittsburgh and Allegheny in relation to the trip, &c.

[After the appointments of officers, a committee, and the passage of resolutions commending the railroad] . . . At half twelve we reached home and thus ended the Excursion – a very gratifying one to all concerned and a very encouraging one to the officers of the Connellsville Road."

Note: The Pittsburgh-Connellsville Railroad had been chartered in 1837. Delays and obstacles prevented the completion of the first section (25 miles) from West Newton to Connellsville until 1855. In 1860, the Fayette County Railroad was completed from Connellsville to Uniontown. By 1871, the former line, finally, completed the track from Uniontown, via Confluence, to Cumberland, Md. In 1875 both railroads in Fayette County were leased to the B&O – and the connection was made with Pittsburgh.

ℒ

— 23 —
Pittsburgh Daily Gazette, February 19, 1857
"PITTSBURGH UNDER A CLOUD.—

Yesterday morning, owing either to the peculiar state of the atmosphere or to an extra amount of smoke in it, we were for about an hour so completely enveloped as to find it difficult to discern an object at the distance of a single square in the more central portions of the city. The 'rock' as they call it in Edinburg[h] seemed to pack down close into the streets, and we discerned men as trees walking. This incense which goes up from the altars of our industry speaks of the great manufacturing and commercial activity of Pittsburgh. But it tells too, rather severely upon our comfort. We would we could have some scheme adopted among our leading mill-owners and thence passed into general use, for the consumption of the smoke as fast as it is made. So much has been said about it, that people have got tired of hearing and talking, and after all it ends in smoke – smoke at night, smoke in the morning, smoke at all hours except perhaps when the vast cloud is driven away for a time before a clear high wind. We do not know what per cent of the volumes which roll from a thousand chimneys in this city would be combustible if submitted to some such process as it is in London, Manchester and other large and smoke cities in England. Very much of it, however, we are confident might be made to minister to our comfort rather than be, as it now is, an ever present nuisance. But of this one discomfort, this would be one of the most charming places in the United States. What grand scenery environs us; where can one find in any other portion of the country more vibrant and romantic hills, so rich and picturesque valleys, more neat and tasteful villas than around this city. Almost the moment we cross the city bounds we are in the midst of a country charming to every scene; which spring clothes with flowers, and autumn enriches with the choicest fruits. Two bright beautiful rivers come down from the mountain lands with the rich freightage of industry, dive into the cloud here and emerge again below, one broad river, a union consummated in accordance with an ancient rite, under a veil, but none the less beautiful or desirable were that removed. As much as we long for the prosperity of the city of our adoption, so earnestly do we wish that this dreadful inconvenience, this mote in our eye, this fly in our ointment, this drop of bitter in our cup of sweet, this – 'in short to use the words of Mr. Micawber,' this smut in your nose, this dirt in our clothes, this omnipresent enemy of our comfort, were expelled, consumed, destroyed, removed and forever abated. So mote it be."

Pittsburgh Daily Gazette, August 7, 1857
"Editorial Correspondence
of the Pittsburgh *Gazette*
FAYETTE SPRINGS, Aug. 4, 1857.

Eds. *Gazette* – Out of the noise and smoke of the city, among the mountains and enjoying their cool breezes, I take a moment to drop you a line. There is nothing in particular to be said out of the usual routine of such letters, but the simple fact of a slight relaxation from the cares and toils which business imposes upon us in the daily walks of life, brings with it so much enjoyment, that it is difficult not to write a letter though it may have in it nothing either instructive or interesting.

The journey hither is very pleasant. Taking the steamer at Pittsburgh, the rich and ever-varying panorama of the Monongahela Valley, the shifting light and shade, the pictures of still life that crowd upon the view and the scenes of activity on the bosom of the river itself, all tend to keep one alive to the beauty which presses upon the eye at every turn. Nor is the scene wanting in historic interest. One always will think of Washington and Braddock and the brave hearts long mouldered into dust, as he passes the fatal field where civilization and barbarism met in their most deadly conflict on our soil and where impracticable military martnetism received its severest blow. As our boat glided along by those peaceful hills it was not difficult to picture to the mind the gorgeous parade of veterans who with brave music and flaunting banner marshaled their way to gory death, 'a hundred years ago' although it was over the very ground where now peace garners her overflowing harvests and plenty smiles at a thousand fire-sides. The contrast is significant; both the one and the other are types of their age: each an epitome of their respective eras: the age of conquest passing and of conquest perfected. But our boat moves on; a sudden bend in the river and we are at Brownsville 'a city set upon a hill,' where an evident struggle has been making between the rural and the urban, where ambitious streets have been encroached upon by avaricious meadows and cornfields and wide sweeps of golden grain. It is a pleasant quiet place looking down upon the river in front and from the summit of the hill whose side it occupies, commanding a view of meadow, village, stream, harvest-field, grove, valley and mountain which one never tires in looking upon. – As we journey onward to Uniontown each turn in the winding way opens some new view where groves heap up their rich piles of foliage and broad fields of ripe grain wave in the passing breeze. Beyond all, to the eastward, the chain of the Alleghenies makes the background to as charming a picture as can be seen anywhere in the country. I have traveled in the Great West that boasts so much of its wonders of wealth, its rich landscapes, it generous harvest fields, its romantic rivers and its genuine hospitality, but in all these respects it is far behind just this home of ours, this land that encircles our own city, this diversified scene of hill and vale around our own houses as it were. When a farmer sells his own fertile acres here, and, leaving behind him the scenes of his youth, the school house where he was trained, and the church in which his fathers worshipped, goes to some place in the West, how much does he gain? Does he buy his fuel with his new farm? Does he find brighter skies, purer air, more wholesome water, a life better calculated to enkindle land to cherish the holier aspirations of the heart, better society, better schools or indeed even a more generous soil? There can be but one answer to those questions. The great world of the West must be subdued to civilization; that is admitted. But that world is for those to go in and possess who have yet homes to make for themselves like those which the fathers have already made here; for young men who disfigure the corners of the streets in our cities or earn a precarious living in some shop doing work which women could do with far greater advantage.

But while I speculate I ride and am at Fayette Springs. A journey on horseback over the winding mountain road is a thing to be enjoyed like welcome rest after anxious toil; and a fine comfortable house at the end of the ride, a house large clean and airy, nestling among the shady trees under the shoulders of the mountains, and our pleasant host, Babcock to bid you welcome – that is comfort concentration that is romance made reality; that is like the shadow of the rock in a weary land.

I found a large company of Pittsburghers at the hotel – Judge Hampton and family, Mr. Coleman and family, Mr. Warner and family, Mr. Rhodes the artist, and others to the number of thirty or forty, all enjoying themselves in this quiet retreat. The tide of whisky-drinkers does not set in this direction and those who would enjoy truly a rural retreat undisturbed by fashionable follies, or the exhibitions of those grosser forms of vice, always made where there are invitations to the reckless and intemperate to gratify their morbid thirst, will do well to pay this place a visit. There are no such invitations here, and the day and evening are passed in walking and riding, or in the enjoyment of music or a social hop at night. Here are the groves, -- 'Gods first temples,' the ever arching blue of the sky, the shaggy mountain ridges closing up the horizon on all sides and breathing upon you the cool fresh breath from 'gurgling brooks and leafy fastnesses.' I have enjoyed every moment since I have been here and with many regrets must bid adieu to all those comforts and take up the line of march for the hot pavements and the smoke of the Iron City.

There are several routes by which the traveler may reach here. The one I chose to take was by the steamer to Brownsville, thence through Uniontown to this place. Distance to Brownsville, 60 miles; thence to Uniontown, 12 miles; thence to 'the Springs' over the mountain on the excellent road, 8 miles. The tourist will enjoy no part of it better than the trip on the river. But this letter is tedious and I stop here.[1] D.L.E."

❧

— 25 —

Pittsburgh Daily Gazette, August 4, 1858
"(Correspondence of the Pittsburgh *Gazette*)
THE MONONGAHELA LANDING AT PITTSBURGH

A contract, it seems, has been made for the paving of that portion of our city which lies between Water street and the Monongahela river, and extending from the Point, or junction of our two rivers up to that portion which has already been graded and paved.

We have now, and for many years past have had, a very extensive landing place, sufficient for the accommodation of a large number of steamboats, and I believe I have heard it spoken of as the most extensive and commodious in the Great Valley. This project for the extension of the grading

---

[1]Fayette Springs Hotel opened in 1814, after a Uniontown physician, Daniel Marchand, determined that the mineral waters had curative qualities. It was a very popular resort for the elite. The main hotel burned in 1879; but it continued a limited operation until the 1890s.

and paving very naturally recalls the attention of an old resident to the condition of the landing during his childhood and early manhood. The change that he has witnessed during a half century, in the appearance of that portion of our city, is truly remarkable, and probably very many of our citizens who daily transact a large business with the steamboats with such great facility, be means of this improvement, have no conception of the change which time and money have produced in this quarter.

Fifty years ago, and even at a later day, there was no such convenience at Pittsburgh as a graded bank or paved landing place. The south side of Water street was rugged and broken. The descent to the water of the Monongahela instead of being a regular grade, as it is now, was by a steep, broken bank, such as may be seen any place along the river where the hand of man has not interfered to arrest and correct the ravages of high water. The width of that portion of Water street above the beach was of various breadths at different points.

During a prosecution for nuisance which I will hereafter have occasion to refer to, it became proper to have an accurate measurement of the breadth of Water street from the line of the houses to the break of the bank. The measurement was made by Alexander Johnson, Jr., and William Crawford, the Street Commissioner. I had for many years their statement in my hands, but handed it over to my successor when I resigned the City Solicitorship. I think, however, I am not mistaken in saying at Grant street and down to near Wood street it was from sixty-eight to fifty feet wide, and the bank was high and abrupt. At Wood street there was a drain, up which the river, when high, backed above Front street, so that at a very early day a bridge was built across the drain to enable persons to pass up Front street, from Wood towards Smithfield. From Wood street down to

Redoubt alley the distance from the house to the break of the bank would average about fifty feet, except that at Market street, a gulley with steep, almost perpendicular banks, ran so close to the houses as to prevent two wagons passing each other; at Chancery lane another gulley overreached so far as to render it impassable even by a single wagon, and at the mouth of Ferry street great care was necessary in passing. At the south of Redoubt alley stood the Redoubt built by Col. Wm. Grant in 1765. It stood on the verge of the bank, and being about twenty-two feet square there was barely room for a wagon to pass between it and the corner post of the lot on which John Irwin's warehouse now stand. From the west side of Redoubt alley there was a rapid descent going towards the point for about sixty or seventy feet. At this point a drain came in, which, no doubt, had once been a run or an outlet for a considerable flow of water; this drain was, probably, impassable in times of moderately high water; but at period before my recollections sewer had been constructed extending from Front street to a point eighteen or twenty feet beyond the south line of lot of Water street. From this drain or sewer to Short street wagons could pass – westward on Short street, along Water, wagons never went. The distance from the line of the lots to the break of the bank, between Short and West streets, was no where more than twenty feet and a part of the distance it was not five. All this distance from Grant street to West, Water street was bounded on one side by the abrupt bank, except at two or three places where sideling ways were made to the river, or where, as at Wood street, a drain came in and wore away the high bank. On the west side of West street James O'Hara's fence of lot No. 145 extended down the bank, (which here was sloping) on to the beach, so that there was no direct communication by wagon or carriage along Water street between the mouth of Liberty and that of West or Short; but a man with a load of coal landing at the end of Liberty street and going to a house at the corner of Water and Short, must drive by Liberty to Front, up Front to Short and then along Short back to Water street.

C."

PITTSBURGH IN 1859.
Source: *Fleming's View of Old Pittsburgh.*

26

Pittsburgh Daily Gazette, August 12, 1858
"(Correspondence of the *Pittsburgh Gazette)*
NEAR BRADY'S BEND, August 9, 1858

Dear *Gazette:* We formed one of a small party of health and pleasure seekers which left the din and dust of the city a few days ago since, to find, in the rustic shadow of Armstrong [County], that quiet, purity of atmosphere and rural abandon, which is the secret of the improved appetite and healthy complexion, which a few weeks in the country is apt to produce.

We were surprised to find so goodly a number of passengers on the A[llegheny] V[alley Railroad] train on the morning of our departure. Conductor Alexander is a courteous, careful, and popular gentleman, a favorite with the traveling public, and hence, we presume, the fact that he had all the passengers he could seat in two first class cars.[1]

How we sniffed the pure air, when once fairly outside the city; how we admired the panorama of the beautiful Allegheny [River], its leaf-clad hills, its fairy islands, and its wild, romantic dells! Above Hulton, our attention was first attracted by Crosson, a beautiful farm villa, belonging to mine host of the Monongahela House, and where he cultivates vegetables good enough in quantity and quality to serve up the palatial table of his great hotel. It is a lovely place, and will attract the eye of travelers close by; on the south side of the road is another fine property, belonging to Mr. Edward Grier, who has surveyed the premises, so as to divide into pleasant building lots, sloping gently toward the

---

[1]The Allegheny Valley Railroad was completed to Kittanning (Mile 56) in 1856.

road and rivers. Here there is a fountain at play, tossing its sparkling jet in the morning sun, and producing miniature rainbows free gratis to the admiration of the passing traveler. Mr. Grier has taken captive a mountain spring, some distance above, which, conducted down in pipes, here rejoins in its freedom from restraint by leaping high in the air, and tumbling in a copious and perpetual shower into an imaginary grotto full of rocks and moss, shells, gold-fish, etc.

Logan's bottom, across the river, next attracts the eye, sweeping around a promontory formed by a bend in the river. Close by, a little further up, on the right, is the flourishing village of Parnassus, with its dozen new houses and its pleasant surroundings. There we shriek out at Tarentum, Freeport, and halt at the Katanyan [Kittanning] as the natives call their county town. Here we encountered several members of the 'Mary Ann' fishing club, in their red flannel shirts, full of piscatorial excitement, but more anxious for a *Gazette*. Our friend W., who had laid down his pestle and abandoned his mortar to seize the fishing pole, procured a copy of your 'morning edition' from the news boy, and started for the 'Mary Ann' in triumph, giving us a kind invitation to visit them at our convenience.

Having quite a goodly number of women and children under our charge for the time (we have but one wife and baby ourselves,) we felt a commendable anxiety in regard to the accommodations of Messrs. Lightcap and Piper, for the balance of the trip of 18 miles. They have such a curious habit, these stagers, of charging you a half seat for babies, without making any after calculations for the aforesaid, in the apportionment of seats. As near as our memory serves us, we had nine children to stow away in our stage, after it was full of children of larger growth. But were we not going to the country, and should we not conform to its customs?

En route to Brady's Bend, there are several points worthy of note. One eminence is so high that from its summit you look away off in [a] South-east direction to the blue tops of the Allegheny Mountains, and away off yonder is the distant horizon, South-west, a range of blue topped hills which our jehu [a fast driver] informs us are in the immediate neighborhood of Pittsburgh.

The crops, generally, are good. Oats are partially rusted, but will yield a fair crop. Wheat is middling, potatoes and corn good, and fruit, of all kinds a failure. There are plenty of blackberries – some almost as fine looking as the Lawton – and any quantity of whortleberries.

How we have good a fishing, what we caught, how we went berrying, what we found, and how we procured horses and saddles and give the ladies a lesson in equestrianism – together with various experiments in dance aquatics, sometimes called 'paddling my own canoe,' but without the poetical meaning, we may tell you in another letter.

Yours,
RUSTIS"

27

Pittsburgh Daily Gazette, November 23, 1858
"CENTENNIAL CELEBRATION
Centennial Anniversary
of the Evacuation of Fort Duquesne
[during the 'French and Indian War'] —
November 25th, 1758

The Committee of Arrangements, in connection with the Chief Marshal and Aids, have arranged the following programme for the Centennial Celebration on Thursday next:

The Committee of Arrangements for celebrating this most interesting of the historical events of Western Pennsylvania, in perchance of the duties of their appointment, announce that most extensive arrangements have been made for commemorating, in a becoming manner, that interesting event, on Thursday, November 25th, 1858, in the city of Pittsburgh, and expect that the procession will be perhaps the most imposing demonstration of the kind ever witnessed in our State.

The Officers of the day chosen are:

President – Hon. Wm. Wilkins

Vice-Presidents – Allegheny county- Neville B. Craig, Hon. H. M. Breckinridge, Hon. George Darsie, Col. Wm. G. Hawkins, Hilary Brunot, Esq., John Thaw, Esq., Major Wm. Graham, Jr., Hon. Charles Shaler, Wm. Eichbaum, Esq., John Snyder, Esq., Hon. Wm. F. Johnston, Sylvanus Lothrop, Esq., John Graham, Esq., James Anderson, Esq., John Anderson, Esq., Thomas Bakewell, Esq., John Irwin, Esq., J. Brown, Esq., J. Beitler, Esq., John Sampson, Esq., J. D. Davis, Esq.

Westmoreland county – Alexander Johnston, Frederick J. Cope, Gen. Wm. A. Stokes, John C. Plummer, Esq.

Fayette county – Hon. J. L. Dawson, Hon. Andrew Stuart, James Veech, Esq.

Washington county -- Col. Wm. Hopkins, Hon. J. Ewing, Hon. J. Knight.

Greene county – Jesse Lazier, Esq., Gen. J. H. Wells

Beaver county – Hon. D. Agnew, Geo. Shoras, Esq.

Butler county – J. Mechling, Esq. D. Dongal, Esq.

Mercer county – Hon. Wm. Stewart, John Leech, Esq.

Lawrence county – David Sankey, Esq., J. Kisslek, Esq.

Crawford county – Hon. John Dick, John M'Farland, Esq.

Erie county – Hon. J. Thompson, M. Babbitt, Esq.

Venango county – Hon. A. Plummer, R. Irwin.

Warren county – G. C. Irwin, Esq.

Jefferson county – J. H. Bell, Esq., A. Caryler [?], Esq.

Elk county – Hon. J. L. Gillis, Judge Dickinson.

Indiana county – Hon. T. White, D. Stewart, Esq.

Clarion county – Hon. C. Myers, Patrick Kerr, Esq.

Blair county – John T. Mathias, Esq., Hon. S. S. Blair.

Cambria county – C. W. Pershing, Esq., Hon. P. Noon.

Armstrong county – Hon. J. Buffington, Gen. R. Orr.

Secretaries – Col. Wilson McCandless, John Harper, Esq., Col. James P. Barr, R. Biddle Roberts, Esq., Chas. W. Ricketson, Esq., James B. Murry, Esq., I. O. Hepburn, George Fortune, Esq., Col. Wm. H. Smith, Geo. W. Cass, Esq., Chas. B. Scully, Esq., Henry Lambert, Esq., Col. T. A. Scott, Col. J. Heron Foster, Col. J. P. Glass.

Chief Marshal – Gen. William Robinson, Jr.

Aids to Chief Marshal – Gen. McK. Snodgrass, Col. Samuel M'Kelvy, Capt. C. W. Batchelor, Col. David A. Stewart, John D. Bailey, Robert H. Patterson, Gen. Joseph Markle, Col. W. J. Morrison, Hon. Jonas R. M'Clintock, Robert B. Simpson, M. D., Max K. Moorhead, J. G. Beckofen.

A general invitation is hereby extended to the citizens of Eastern and Western Pennsylvania, Ohio, and Western Virginia, to join with the citizens of Pittsburgh in this celebration. – John S. Cosgrave, Chairman.

-- Order of Procession --

This order of procession, and locality of each delegation, will be as follows:

Military, under command of Gen. Snodgrass, the right resting on Penn and Wayne streets, extending east.

Soldiers of 1812, and the Scott Legion, will form on Wayne street, right resting on Penn street.

Agricultural Society will form on Liberty and Smithfield streets, right resting on Wayne streets, extending down Smithfield street.

United States officers, the Governors of Pennsylvania and Ohio, Mayor of the City of Pittsburgh, and President of the day.

Judges of the Supreme Court of the United States and Pennsylvania, Chaplain and Orator of the day, will form on Smithfield street, right resting on Seventh street.

The Mayor and Councils of Allegheny city, Birmingham, East Birmingham, South Pittsburgh, West Pittsburgh, Temperanceville, Manchester, Lawrenceville, Duquesne borough, Sharpsburg and Pittsburgh, will form on Smithfield street, right resting on Fifth street.

Firemen will form on Duquesne way and Wayne street, right resting on Penn street.

Musical, historical and literary societies will form on Liberty street, right resting opposite the mouth of Smithfield street.

Schools, and delegations of boys, will form on Hand, Liberty and Wood streets, the right resting on Penn street.

Black and White Smiths will form on Sixth street, the right resting on Wood street.

Rolling Mill Men, Steel Manufacturers and Copper Mill Men will form on Ross street, right resting on Fifth street.

Clothiers will form on Wood street, right resting on Sixth street.

Carpenters and Cabinet Makers will form on Wood street, right resting on Wood street and Virgin alley.

Brickmakers, Bricklayers and Roofers will form on Fifth street, right resting on Wood and Fifth streets.

Painters, Plasterers and Paper Hangers will form on Wood street, right resting on Fourth street.

Printers will form on Fourth street, right resting on Wood street.

Cordwainers and Hatters will form on Irwin street, right resting on Penn street.

Copper, Tin and Sheet Iron Manufacturers, will form on Liberty street, the right resting on the corner of Liberty and Irwin streets, line extending up Liberty street.

Butchers will form on Irwin street, north side, resting on Irwin street.

Tanners, Curders [?] and Leather Dealers, will form on Liberty streets, extending down Liberty.

Saddle, Harness and Trunk Makers will form on Liberty street, right resting on Liberty street and Barker's alley.

Chandlers will form on Duquesne way, from Hand street to Irwin street, right resting on Irwin street.

Glass Blowers will form on St. Clair and Market streets, right resting on Penn.

Boiler Makers will form on Market street, right resting on fifth.

Engine Builders and Machinists will form on Market street, right resting on the corner of Market and Fourth streets.

118

Brass Founders will form on Market street, right resting on Second street.

Foundry Men will form on Pitt and Liberty street, right resting on Penn.

Novelty Works will form on First, right resting on Ross [?].

Coal Men and Coal Diggers will form on Ferry street, right resting on Liberty.

Coalboat Pilots and Coalboat Hands will form on Fourth street, right resting on Ferry.

Steamboatmen and Steamboat Builders will form on Second street, right resting on Grant.

Gymnastic Association will form on Diamond street, right resting on Smithfield street.

Railroad Men will form on Third street, right resting on Grant.

Draymen will form on Duquesne way, right resting on Pitt street, extending to St. Clair street bridge.

Charitable, Benevolent and other Associations will form on Pitt street and Duquesne way, right resting on the corner of Penn and Pitt streets.

Along the line of the procession, especially, and throughout the city, generally, it is hoped that our citizens will make a display of banners and flags appropriate to the occasion.—Wm. Robinson, [Chief Marshall].

The Assistant Marshals, and Marshals of Delegations, will meet at the Mayor's Office this evening, at seven o'clock. By order of the Chief Marshal.—Samuel M'Kelvy, C. W. Batchelor, Wm. J. Morrison, Aids —

* * * * * * *

Pittsburgh Morning Post, November 24, 1858

Note: The same information appeared in the *Pittsburgh Morning Post* as in the *Pittsburgh Daily Gazette*, the previous day (November 23, 1858) with the exception of the following closing comments.

"Delegations from the adjoining counties will form on the north side of Liberty street, between Wayne and Washington streets.

SPECIAL ORDERS

Aids to the Chief Marshal will wear blue sashes.

Marshals of Delegations will wear white sashes.

Assistants to Marshals of Delegations will wear red sashes.

It is ordered that no fire-arms shall be carried in the procession, except by the military.

ROUTE OF PROCESSION

The procession will form on Penn and Wayne streets, and proceed down Penn to Marbury, up Marbury to Liberty, down Liberty to Water, up Water to Smithfield, up Smithfield to Liberty, up Liberty to Wayne, down Wayne to Penn, up Penn to Mechanics, down Mechanics and across the bridge to Chesnut, up Chesnut to Ohio, down Ohio to Water lane, along the west side of West Common to Ridge street, up Ridge to Water, up Water to Federal, down Federal and across the bridge to St. Clair, along St. Clair to Liberty, and down Liberty to the Duquesne Depot. – William Robinson, Jr., Chief Marshal.

* * * * * * *

THE CELEBRATION

The arrangements for the celebration tomorrow are very complete. The gentlemen on the several committees have performed their duties with great good sense. The public interest in the occasion has been excited in a high degree, and there is no doubt that the proceedings tomorrow will be on a magnificent scale, and creditable to our city. We refer to our advertising columns for detailed statements of the various orders of the day.

The oration at the Duquesne Depot, by Hon. Andrew W. Loomis, and the Ode by F. B. Plympton, Esq., set to music by Harry Kleber, will be two of the features of the day. The ode is to be sung by the Amateurs of our city, and the German Frohsinn and Teutonia Musical Societies, aided by a good orchestra.

The following is a copy of the ode:

'ONE HUNDRED YEARS AGO

I.

One hundred years ago to-day,
  In martial state the heroes came,
To plant within the wilderness,
  Their grand old English name and fame.
They saw the glory of the land,
  The realm of nations yet to be,
And rescued from the allied for
  The empire of the free.
      United thus, may Saxon fire,
        And sons forever meet the foe
      And strike for Freedom as they struck,
        One hundred years ago.

II.

One hundred years have passed – and Peace
  In golden fullness o'er us reigns,
Full Plenty smiles on all our hills,
  And Gladness sings in all our plains.
The flag of freemen greet the air
  Where waved the standard of our sires,
And all their altars still are bright
  With Freedom's sacred fires.
      Here Fame shall keep a holy trust,
        The names of those who met the foe,
      And won for us this glorious land
        One hundred years ago.

III.

So aid us, Heaven, to keep our trust,
  That in the coming centuries,
They'll say, Where truth and valor live
  The light of Freedom never dies.
God of our Fathers, keep us still
  The chosen people of Thy hand,
One in our fealty to thee,
  One to our native land.
      O, guide us, while we watch and guard,
        From inward strife and outward foe,
      The heritage so nobly won,
        One hundred years ago."

28

Pittsburgh Daily Gazette, May 12, 1860
"THE FLOOD.

Quite a throng of people crowded the pavements along the wharves of both rivers yesterday, to see the immense freshet which the late rains have produced. From the indications at that time it seemed the flood would rival that of '52 and perhaps even reach as high as that of '32. The rivers continued rising the whole day, during the morning the Allegheny at the rate of about 5 inches an hour. The Monongahela, we think, did not swell so rapidly. The wharves presented an excited scene, the freight being huddled together in close contact to remove it from the constant approach of the water, and all the boats that were receiving cargoes having the largest available force employed to store away in the hold what was intended for shipment. The hull of the steamboats at the mouth of Wood street could be seen from almost any square between Water and Liberty streets, and it looked very much as if they were going to run up the street and form a communication by water between our prominent business houses and the wharf. We believe, in the flood of '32, the water came as far perhaps as Second street, but consequent pavings have no doubt made Wood street higher than it was then. At the Point a number of houses were inundated, the water reaching some distance into the first story, but how high we were only able to conjecture, as we could not get near enough to make an estimate. Four flat boats were sunk a hundred feet below the bridge, and it was reported the men on board were drowned. This, however, was incorrect. They were all saved, one man by climbing up the brush and drift that had lodged against the pier, from which he was rescued by persons on the bridge. A number of coal boats, we understand, passed over the dams on the Monongahela slackwater. The pier mark on the Monongahela bridge registered about 33 ft. at 6 o'clock yesterday evening. The Allegheny river began to rise on Monday morning, and has steadily continued to do so until the present time. On Tuesday afternoon, the residents in the lower part of Allegheny, known as the 'Bottom,' began to move out their household goods, in anticipation of a flood similar to that of '52. In the evening about 8 o'clock, 'Smoky Island' was completely under water, and the cellars and the first stories of many houses in the lower part of Allegheny were filled with water. The water in the channel of the Allegheny river at dark on Tuesday, as shown by the 'mark,' was 25 feet. The river that night kept steadily rising until 5 o'clock, Wednesday morning, at the rate of 8 inches an hour; after that, until midnight last night, at the rate of 3 1/2 inches an hour. At an early hour (6 o'clock) on Wednesday morning, the families living on the river bank, saw that an inundation was inevitable, and began to move their furniture to the upper stories of their dwelling, and prepare for the worst, and at 9 o'clock yesterday morning, most of the residences from the river up to Robinson street were flooded, that of Sol. Schoyer, Esq., being completely isolated from the rest of the city by the surrounding water, the only means of communication being by means of boats. – The water continued to rise at the rate of an inch and three quarters an hour until our paper went to press.

The water at 9 1/2 o'clock yesterday morning had reached Lacock street, by way of Craig, and the people were moving out by boats. At 10 o'clock it was within three feet of the mark of the '52 flood. At 11 o'clock it reached Robinson street, by way of Sandusky street.

On the Pittsburgh side of the river, at 12 o'clock the water had reached the steps of the Ferry and Scott Houses, and the steamboats *Venango* and *Allegheny Belle, No. 2,*[1] were anchored within 25 yards of the Scott House, to the fire plug on the corner of Hancock and Duquesne Way. This is the most disastrous flood that has occurred since '52, and it will take thousands of dollars to repair the damage it has already done.

Among the numerous instances of quick moving we heard, was that of Mercer and Robinson; a party of six gentlemen, friends of theirs, hearing that the firm anticipated the river would rise Tuesday night, and destroy a large quantity of salt they had stored in a warehouse on the Canal basin, volunteered their assistance to help remove it; they commenced at 11 o'clock that night, and by daylight Wednesday morning had succeeded in moving up on the common, several hundred barrels; just as they finished the water commenced to rush through the door.

At 8 o'clock last night, the water was rising more rapidly than at any other time in the afternoon. The water was four feet and a half high in the Penn Cotton Mill. A large pile of 2 1/2 inch plank, probably 10 feet high, passed the suspension bridge in the afternoon, not a plank was displaced.

Quite an animated scene was presented by the people moving by skiffs, men and boys on rafts, poleing around, and every now and then falling in and getting a cold bath.

---

[1]The small 120-ton *Venango* was built in 1858 in California, Pa. Designed for the Pittsburgh-Franklin trade on the Allegheny, she ran there during the "oil excitement" until 1862, when she was sold down the Ohio. She burned in Louisiana in 1864. The *Allegheny Belle No. 2* was built at Brownsville in 1850. She, too, ran on the Allegheny River trade until being dismantled in 1860.

Crowds of both sexes were on the suspension bridge watching affairs.

At 12 o'clock last night, the atmosphere was clear and cool, the stars shining brightly, and no appearance of any more rain."

&

— 29 —
Pittsburgh Daily Gazette, June 18, 1861
"A VISIT TO PITTSBURGH

The Editor of the Washington *Star* has been 'on the wing' westward, and lately visited Pittsburgh, about which, as 'a chief among us takin[g] notes,' perhaps some of our readers will not be averse to hear him.

From Altoona my way lay for the first thirteen miles up the mountains. In that distance the [Pennsylvania] railroad ascends here eleven hundred feet, and at one point doubles on its tracks, as it were, almost as short as the crook of one's elbow. Though grand and interesting, the country in the mountain here is by no means as stupendous and striking as that greeting the eye of the traveler upon the mountain section of the Baltimore and Ohio Railroad. The difficulties of the location and construction of this road over the Alleghenies were not a tithe of those of the other. That is, in crossing the great backbone of the Atlantic country. I reached Pittsburgh shortly after noon, traveling from the top of the mountain- where there is a watering place called Cresson – almost entirely through a cultivated and thickly inhabited region. Though few elaborate farm improvements were visible from the car window on either hand, thrift, abundance and intelligent agriculture were visible in all the surroundings by the way. The descent to the head of the Ohio river at Pittsburgh was rapid and agreeable. Seven or eight east of Pittsburgh I passed the celebrated site of Braddock's defeat—marked in no especial manner to distinguish it from surrounding fields. From that point to Pittsburgh the country is devoted to elegant villas and private mansions, as well appointed in all respects as those of any other American city's suburbs.

At Pittsburgh, the [Civil] war again obtruded itself forcibly upon my observation. The fair grounds and buildings were occupied by drilling troops, for the most part uniformed, preparing evidently to depart shortly to take part in the coming momentous struggle. As dingy as the all-pervading bituminous smoke makes all Pittsburgh, it is nevertheless a very handsome city, everywhere except in localities devoted to manufacturing only. The stars and stripes seemed to be flying from half of Pittsburgh's thousand of houses. The Union feeling is intense here – as well it may be; for the success of the [Confederate] oligarchy's conspiracy against the integrity of the Union, so far, as struck a blow at Pittsburgh's commerce by means of the Mississippi, such as few cities have as yet experienced. Doubtless her available dollar and men will be freely accorded to restore the authority of the United States over the States professing to have seceded. Her only hope for the future – the immediate future, I mean – rests upon the maintenance of the Union at any cost and at all hazard; and, the Star's readers may rely on it, she (Pittsburgh) is 'in the war' with almost appalling earnestness and energy.

To-day she can command more actual money and men for its prosecution than the whole State of South Carolina, though her actual population may not be more than 150,000; her resources of men being, in addition to her own at present unemployed laborers and mechanics, thousands and tens of thousands Ohio river men usually making their break in connection with the transportation of her heretofore so extensive manufactures and the raw materials out of which her immediate population fashions them. Her bridges connecting Pittsburgh proper with her newest half – Allegheny City – are remarkably fine structures – four in number – spanning the Allegheny in the vicinity of each other, and connecting the two divisions of the city by four principal streets of either. The Allegheny city wards are most sought of late for the construction of residences of Pittsburgh's merchant princes – to achieve space for their proper surroundings, as well as exemption from the all pervading nuisance of coal dust and tar, which, in a single season, turns red bricks black, or white paint almost black, in the midst of Pittsburgh's tall manufacturing chimneys.

According to the estimate of an intelligent citizen riding by [my] side, the war has already cost Pittsburgh the loss of a third of her late vast commerce; or in other words, of well nigh a third of her really vast wealth, carried by hard labor and intelligent enterprise in the last fifty years. That she will fight to the bitter end for its recovery, and will freely spend all the rest in the effort to recover it, is as certain as that the sun will rise to morrow or one may draw unjust conclusions from the writer's history of the civil war of other nations."

❧

Pittsburgh Daily Gazette,
Monday, September 30, 1861
"ANOTHER FLOOD – GREAT DESTRUCTION OF
PROPERTY

The constant and heavy rains of Thursday night and Friday were followed by an unusually sudden rise in our rivers, which continued until they attained flood hight, causing immense destruction of property along the Allegheny and Monongahela valleys, and inundating portions of both cities and surrounding boroughs. The rain ceased to fall about ten o'clock Friday night, having continued to pour down in torrents for about thirty hours. Both rivers began to swell before the rain ceased, and during Friday night the pier-mark indicated a rise of fifteen feet. At noon on Saturday the depth in channel was twenty-six and a half feet, and at eleven o'clock Saturday night – when the rain ceased – the depth was <u>thirty feet nine and a half inches.</u> The water was only nine inches below the memorable inundation of 1852, and almost three feet less than the 'great flood of 1832'– the greatest ever known to the inhabitants.

The present flood happened at an unusual season of the year, and was not anticipated by many – hence the destruction of floating property was greater than it might otherwise have been. Immense quantities of lumber, including sawed lumber, logs, shingles, etc., have been swept from the Allegheny river and its tributaries, most of which will be entirely lost to the owners. Among the articles observed hurrying down the current, were barns, sheds, out-houses, sections of bridges, broken rafts, bundles of shingles, and pine logs innumerable. All these foot up a very heavy loss, though it be divided among thousands of owners. Judging from the endless number of pumpkins and squashes, which floated gaily down the streams, our worthy farmers on the river and creek bottoms will lack 'some pumpkins' this winter.

On the Monongahela, the loss was principally confined to the coal business. A large number of empty barges was swept from their moorings, and either dashed to pieces or carried into the Ohio. W.H. Brown is the heaviest loser in this respect – a great many of the barges bearing his initials. He also lost a loaded barge, which was wrecked against a pier of the Birmingham bridge. The quantity of drift wood and debris which came down this river was also very large, though not of a valuable character.

The damage in and around the two cities is not of a very serious character. There were no valuable fleets of coal boats awaiting shipment to the South, and but very little lumber at our landings. The bridges all escaped injury, although some apprehensions were felt for the safety of the Mechanics' street, or 'upper bridge,' owing to the immense pressure brought against some of the piers by the accumulated drift wood. The water raised to within two or three feet of the superstructure of most of the bridges, but they all stood firm. The wire cables of the old [canal] aqueduct, which were in process of removal from the piers, had sunk so low between two of the piers as to catch the drift wood – an immense pile of which is now visible, and still accumulating so rapidly that it is feared either the cables or the piers will have to yield to the pressure. A portion of the cap of one of the piers has already given way, but the cable fell and rested upon the body of the pier. The drift wood extends some two hundred and fifty or three hundred feet up the river, in a compact mass, reaching some eight or ten feet out of the water. If it should give way, it may endanger the piers of some of the bridges below.

The railroad trains diverging from this city, (excepting the Allegheny Valley Railroad), escaped uninjured, and are making their trips as usual. On the Allegheny Valley road considerable damage was done, and it was reported that a bridge had been swept away.

Navigation on the Allegheny and Monongahela river has been suspended, the boats being unable to pass under the bridges until the water subsides.

Those 'unfortunate' people residing on the low ground in the First and Fourth wards, Allegheny, have been in a most pitiable condition for the past thirty-six hours, and hundreds of them are not yet released from the watery siege. Whole acres of houses are surrounded by water, and in scores of instances the water reached the second story. Communication with the dry portions of the city was had by skiffs, when these small craft could be obtained, but generally by the rudest specimen of raft, upon which those who could not keep a perfect balance did not dare to venture. Rich and poor, old and young, sick and well . . . all shared the same fate, and many incidents, serious as well as comic, might be told of the flood. As there are some three or four editors among the 'submerged,' we may yet have some incidents from them – jokes which we may reasonably expect will not be dry.

In this city, from the Point, all along the bank of the Allegheny to the city line, the water found its way into hundreds of dwellings, and in Sharpsburg, Stewartstown, Duquesne Borough, Manchester, Woods Run, Lawrenceville, Brownstown, Birmingham, Braddocks—field, South and West Pittsburgh, Monongahela Borough and Temperanceville, the houses skirting the river had to entertain the same unwelcome visitor. But, so far as we have been able to learn, no lives were lost in either city, and no serious accident happened.

The water remained at a stand from eleven o'clock Saturday night till four o'clock Sunday morning, when it began to recede, leaving behind, on street, and garden, and floor, a thick covering of dirty, slimy sand – most detestable in the eyes of housewives.

We learn from a gentleman who arrived on Saturday night from up the Allegheny, that the destruction along the Clarion river was very great. Nearly all the lumber on that stream was carried off, and numerous saw mills were swept away. Five saw mills were counted near the south of Clarion river, at one time, and the lumber entered the Allegheny in a perfect gorge. Our informant states that he saw at least 1,000,000 feet of lumber pass down the stream in a short time – being principally in broken sections or rafts.

On the Kiskiminetas river the destruction was also great. The bridge over this river at Leechburg, Armstrong Co., was swept away, and much other damage was done.

All the tributaries of the Allegheny swelled very rapidly, and we fear that the details of the loss will present a frightful aggregate."

31

Pittsburgh Daily Gazette, Friday, November 3, 1865
"MEMORANDA OF [A FISHING TRIP ON]
STEAMER *FORT PITT* [1]

Left Pittsburgh on the 23d ult.[last] at 8:30 a.m.; took
Capt. Bachelor on board at Lock No. 2, [Mile 11] and arrived
at McKeesport at 11:30 a.m. Left McKeesport at 1:30 p.m.,
and arrived at dam No. 1 on the Youghiogheny river at 3:00
p.m. Towed up two flat boat loads of stone, and repaired the
dam, before we were able to get through the lock. Was at
dam No. 1 all day Tuesday hunting and fishing; found the
water too deep for fishing, and the hills too high for hunting.
Wednesday morning the party took the skiff, and went up to
dam No. 2, a distance of nine miles. Fished there all day,
taking 35 pounds of fish, among which was a salmon nearly
three feet in length, weighing about 14 pounds. On the
return trip, met the boat, and ran up to Osceola, where we
laid up for the night. Thursday morning we started down,
and stayed at dam No. 2 until 2 o'clock, and then ran down
to McKeesport, arriving there at 4:30 p.m. Laid there for a
few minutes, and ran up to lock No. 4 [present-day North
Charleroi], where we stayed all night. Friday morning we
started for dam No. 6, or Rice's landing, [Mile 68.5] arriving
at 9 p.m. having arrived at Brownsville that afternoon at 5
o'clock, where we stopped for a few minutes. At Rice's landing the citizens turned out en mass, and the party were es-
corted up town, where after having serenaded the town
(some of the party being musically inclined, and furnished
with instruments) one of the residences was thrown open,

---

[1]The steamer *Fort Pitt* was built, apparently, in Pittsburgh. She
was quite small because she ascended the Beaver Canal at Roches-
ter on the Ohio up to Conneaut Lake where she "wintered and
returned to Pittsburgh April 1866."

and a dance kept up until 2 o'clock in the morning. Saturday morning ran up to Whitel[e]y creek, arriving about 11 o'clock. Hunting and fishing very poor. One of the party suggested that the best game to be found then was the game of poker. Explored the creek, and found plenty of [oil] derricks, but 'nary 'ile.' Left Saturday evening and ran up to Greensborough and [New] Geneva. Laid up at Geneva until the evening of the next day, and then ran up to Cheat river. Sunday night returned to Whitel[e]y Creek. Lay at Whitel[e]y creek next until 2 p.m., and found plenty of ducks and squirrels, but no fishing. Left there at 2 p.m., and arrived at lock No. 4 at 11:30 p.m., where we laid up all night. Left No. 4 at 7:30 a.m. and arrived at [Lock] No. 3 [Mile 25] at 10:30, and at McKeesport at 12:30. Left McKeesport at 2 p.m. and arrived safe and sound at Pittsburgh at 5:30 Monday evening. Our cook was a jewel. We killed and picked two ducks, and [put] them in the pot before they were done kicking. The success of the trip was owing mainly to the efficiency of the pilot and engineer. We offered to rebuild dam No. 2 on the Youghiogheny, but the citizens thought that they had navigation enough.[2] The fun department was conducted by the musicians and party historian."

∾

---

[2]Gen. William Larimer financed the construction of the two locks and dams on the Yough to West Newton, 18.5 miles upriver, during 1848-49. No. 1 was at Boston, 5.5 miles upstream and No. 2 at Buena Vista at Mile 12. Tolls were insufficient, however, and by 1858 the navigation company was broke. The completion of the Pittsburgh and Connellsville Railroad in 1861 left only the coalboat traffic. Coal shippers operated the dams until 1867 when another ice gorge broke the dams beyond repair. Larimer went out west and founded Denver, CO.

32

Pittsburgh Daily Gazette, November 1, 1870
"FAYETTE COUNTY FAIR.

Closing of the Fayette County
Agricultural and Mechanical Fair
(Special Correspondence Pittsburgh *Gazette*)
Brownsville, October 28, 1870

The second annual exhibition of the above closed this evening, and was a decided success.

As your correspondent has been unable to get an official report of all the entries, he will fill the hiatus with a brief reference to the county and fair.

Fayette county, of which this borough is the leading manufacturing town, was made a county from Westmoreland county in 1783, for which fact I am indebted to Goodloe Bowman, a leading citizen of the borough. The county has been making points of interest of historical importance. It was the residence of Col. [William] Crawford, a veteran of the revolution, who served with honor and credit as an officer at the head of an expedition at Sandusky [Ohio] plains. The county also forms an important part in contributing to the well known, but infamous Whiskey Insurrection. Since when has arisen an insurrection so monstrous an extent as to sweep our beloved land with the besom of destruction, and bring wailing and woe to every household, and turn up hundreds of thousands of new made graves has been extinguished in blood and peace and prosperity reign throughout the land. This county contains the remains of the brave but unfortunate [General Edward] Braddock, and is noted for some of the early explo[i]ts of Washington. Queen Allaquippa frequently made visits to 'Red Stone Old Fort,' now

Brownsville, from her wigwams at the mouth of Yough-[iogheny River], and the other at McKee's rocks.[1]

As the successful mechanical inventions it stands prominent. It was here the first wagon brake was invented, now used on every wagon and railroad in the land. The first glass made west of the mountains was made here, and is attributable to that eminent Swiss, the late Albert Gallatin, who for twelve years successfully conducted the portfolio of the United States Treasury of this great nation through a distracted period. Near forty years ago Obed Hussey, the inventor of the open guard, without which no reaper or mower can be successfully used, conceived his first ideas, and absolutely made his first model of this the most important of his field machines with the penknife he used in sharpening pens for his pupils when teaching in an obscure school house. He lived to see this branch of field machinery, his own invention, introduced on over two million of farms. He was killed in the act of doing a kindness to a child, in fact lost his own life to save it. His life was a mission of goodness and his death a martyrdom to his humanity.[2]

Dividing this fantastic Borough from its twin neighbor, Bridgeport, is the first iron bridge ever constructed on the continent. It was planned and built by Gen. G. W. Cass, then almost a youth, and has stood for nearly forty years as

---

[1]Alliquippa was a prominent Seneca woman, a "queen" to the whites, who was pro-English from the early 1700s in eastern Pennsylvania. By the 1730s, she was the head of an Indian community near present-day Pittsburgh. She died in 1754, shortly after Washington's debacle at Ft. Necessity.

[2]Hussey is renowned in the history of agricultural technology. He invented a horse-drawn grain reaper in 1833, while living in Cincinnati, and was the first to patent his invention. He, however, ultimately lost the bitter "reaper battle" with Cyrus McCormick. Hussey may have lived in Fayette County prior to moving to Cincinnati; however, I have been unable to substantiate the writer's comments.

a living monument to the able mechanical and executive skill to one whose success in the conception and construction of the greatest railroad line on the continent, as is well known by your readers is attributable. This bridge crosses Dunlap's Creek a deep steam with a rapid current, and precipitous banks within a few rods of its mouth, where its salubrity is blended into insignificance as it enters the islandless Monongahela.

Other important historical facts and incidents could be given such as the great travel over the mountains by stage on the National Road, when this was regarded as the head of <u>steam boat navigation</u>, . . . The notoriety of the place for steam boat building, &c., are too well known to need your space.

The fair was held about a mile above the village, and was reached by private conveyances. The ground is on the original Krepp's farm whose descendants and lands in the area bear the same to the county that the Robinson and Denney's do in Allegheny county.

The track is a good half [mile?] with a porous, sandy subsoil, which rapidly absorbs moisture. The buildings are new, roomy and well protected. Everything is far above the average of county fairs for convenience, comfort and safety. In this connection the writer takes occasion to say he has attended, in twenty years, two hundred and twenty-three fairs and field trials and has never come across managers and officers who took so much interest in strictly carrying out the conditions of the premium list, and seeing that every exhibitor got fair, impartial justice. The managers are among the wealthiest farmers and business men of Fayette and Washington counties, and are determined to make this a permanent institution; and manage it on first class business principles. I could not see an exhibitor but was satisfied. It is designed to be a respectable place, where the mechanical, agricultural, horticultural and household interests, as well as stock interests, will be represented, and where exhibitors shall have the assurance that it is not a gambling institution, sandwiched between lager beer and pies and coffee. They have wisely excluded all drinking stands and shows without character, and only admit respectable gentlemen with natural living and mechanical curiosity. Like Major Burnell and R. W. Kennedy, or Seven Seal remedy notoriety. Both of these gentlemen were present and were patronized by the best families of the place, and have perfected arrangements for next year.

As I have previously stated, the principal agricultural and mechanical entries were from Pittsburgh and Allegheny City and points west. The old line [of steam] boats made reduced rates and the officers here at the wharf boat. Pittsburgh, also at Brownsville, and Captains and clerks of the different boats did all they could for the convenience of passengers and freight.

Ben Coursin, Esq., one of the directors, and Capt. Adam Jacobs, President of the [Pittsburgh, and Brownsville Packet] line, both old steamboat men, were personally present in aiding the enterprise. Notwithstanding there has never been so large a display left here for an exhibition; there was no confusion, delay or loss.

The Monongahela House over which the late [Civil] war veteran Capt. Krepps presides; the Petroleum, near the [Brownsville] *Clipper* office, under the proprietorship of Isaac Vance, and the Merchants's, under Mrs. Hubbard, were all filled with exhibitors, as was also the Virginia House, managed by Thomas Hopkins in West Brownsville. The guests all speak in the highest terms of the indefatigable efforts of the porters to please and of the reasonable charges.

The premium list was printed by Seth T. Hurd, Esq., editor and proprietor of the [Brownsville] *Clipper* for twenty years. No finer mechanical execution ever (passed?) under my notice. Mr. Hurd, with his paper and personal influence, has for months devoted a great part of his time to the success of the fair.

I have been unable, as remarked at the outset, in naming all the exhibitors in your city and vicinity who have been successful, as there are some books yet out. But of those who are prominent exhibitors are Price, Stewart & Co., 32 and 34 Ohio street, Allegheny city, Major Morton, of the Singer Sewing Machine, Sixth street, whose agent at the point is Mr. Devore and his accomplished lady, who took such an interest in promoting the exhibition, and extended to other competitors every facility for their accommodation.

Captain Hart, of Scenery Hill, Washington county, Pa., who has in connection with his father established the only successful propagating farm in Western Pennsylvania for the production and acclimation of cereals, seeds, esculents [edible foods], &c., received all the principal premiums in this line, as did also W. Herr and wife, of Bentleyville, on farm products and household manufactured goods. Jos. Beckham, of Pittsburgh, the well-known implement dealer received premiums on variety of display, also on fanning mill, corn-shelter, power vegetable cutter, lawn, mower, &c. He is agent. for the 'Continental' hay, straw and fodder cutting box for Western Pennsylvania, also the Buckeye reaper and mower for this county. The latter is too well known to need commendation, as it is the first successful two-wheeled machine ever introduced and has never failed at a State or Horticultural Fair. Mr. James Slocum, of this place, an extensive dealer in machinery and implements, and although contributing extensively to the Fair as an exhibitor, did so, for display and to encourage the enterprise. The 'Continental'" received first premiums at the five State Fairs this fall, besides a large number from different fairs. It is built by the Cleveland Works, owned by Younglove, Massey & Co.

S. Hare & Son, 120 Liberty street, Pittsburgh, exhibited three of the celebrated Champion mower, reaper, and combined self-rake also. These machines have been introduced for some years in this State, and met with a success unparalleled in the history of machinery. One of these was finished for display, to show the elaborate mechanism of the firm, at a cost of some twelve hundred dollars. It was characterized by the thousands who saw it as the finest specimen of workmanship ever offered before the public.

The first premium on combined reaper and mower was awarded the Champion.

S. Hare & Son also successfully exhibited the Red Jack Churn, post-diggers, harrows, cultivators, &c., in which they are extensively engaged. The firm received quite a number of premiums, also, a premium for the largest display of implements. Also, a premium of Spratt's combined hand cultivator and weed exterminator and a patent section grinder. Mr. Hartman, of the firm, was present, and made hosts of friends among farmers and dealers, and received flattering orders.

The Alliance, Ohio, Machine Works received a first premium on their adjustable right and left hand cultivator.

Hussey, Wells & Co., of Pittsburgh, on their steel harrow teeth, used in Spratt, Johnson & Co.'s harrow, received a first premium.

Capt. Espey, on his button hole machine, received a first premium.

T. H. Young, senior member of the firm of T. H. Young & Co., was present and received a first premium on his 'Patent Extension Lounge,' also received a high recommendation from the committee. This was the only article the firm entered, and it created considerable excitement from furniture men, dealers, and others. Besides supplying all the principal boats on this river, the firm in question do large trade in this borough and suburbs, hence it is not surprising Mr. Young received additional orders on the fair ground, and that his work, which is but a sample of furniture daily turned out, received marked attention. I may have seen more elaborate style but certainly never better harmony and style of position. Judge Duncan, an old furniture manufacturer here, highly approved the invention.

J. L. Wise, the book and periodical dealer at this place, has taken every pains to accommodate the public with the latest editions of the *Gazette*. He has been an exhibitor at the fair and received first premiums on his collection of coins which embrace specimens not even found in the mints.

W."[3]

---

[3]The Brownsville Road is still a major, two-lane route south of Pittsburgh. In W. Brownsville, the old route up the hill to California, prior to Route 88, is still designated the Pittsburgh Road.

33

Pittsburgh Daily Gazette, May 10, 1871
"WASHINGTON, PA

A Visit Thither – Anniversary of the Y.M.C. Association –
The Report –President Hay's Address – Railroad Chartier's
Valley – Grain, Fruit, &c.
Pittsburgh, East End, May 8, 1871

I had the pleasure on last Thursday evening, of attending the first Anniversary of the Y.M.C. Association of Washington, Pa. It was held in the Town Hall. The exercises were interesting. They were opened with a voluntary by the Musical Association of the town. Then followed a prayer by the Rev. W.A. Davidson, after this the annual report was read by Freeman Brady, Esq., the President of the Association. The report was a well prepared paper, and showed that a noble work had been done by the Association during the fist year of existence. Religious services had been held weekly in the county jail in the County Home for the Poor, and in the Rooms of the Association; also, two weekly cottage prayer meetings. The Rooms of the Association had been kept open every evening save Sabbath, for the accommodation of young men, where they were supplied with the best of newspaper and magazine reading. In addition to all this, the Association had provided for the town a course of first class lectures, and in so doing had been nobly and generously sustained by the people.

After the reading of the report, Rev. Mr. [George P.] Hays, President of the Washington and Jefferson College, was introduced and made one of his characteristic addresses. It had a good substratum of thought, and then abounded with illustrations and anecdotes, all put in his odd and impressive manner. The audience was well entertained, and the interests of the Association earnestly and ably advocated.

WASHINGTON

It improves a number of buildings going up. Railroads all the talk. Two trains running daily on the Hempfield [Railroad] to and from Wheeling. A strong probability that the road will be, at an early day, completed through on the Connellsville road, making the principal route from Wheeling to Baltimore. The track of the Chartiers [Rail]road is laid within about two miles of Washington. It will be completed in a couple of weeks. Then the Washingtonians purpose a grand celebration. It will be good to be there. Much rejoicing will be had that Pittsburgh at last can be reached by rail.[1]

The Chartiers [Rail]road is being built splendidly. The cars run over it so smoothly that it is a luxury to ride on them. And through what a valley the road runs. Its soil is

---

[1]The Hempfield Railroad Co. was chartered in 1851 under the laws of Virginia to extend from Washington to the Ohio River. It was completed to Wheeling in 1857. It was to extend to Greensburg; some work was done, but it was not finished. In 1871, a vice-president of the Baltimore & Ohio RR purchased it. The B&O Shortline was organized to build from Washington to near Connellsville at Dawson Station. The roadbed of the old Hempfield RR was followed eastward for four miles, and from there to Coal Center where piers were built on the Mon. But, in 1884 the work was suspended. The route would have shortened the distance from Wheeling to the east by many miles. Pittsburgh "interests" may have prevented its construction; which would have lessened the traffic through that city. Two of the three original piers are still standing at Coal Center. What technology!

The Chartiers RR route, between Washington to near Pittsburgh, was surveyed in 1833 but not chartered until 1853. Long delays continued but with the support of the Pennsylvania Railroad, the railway was formerly opened on May 18, 1871 — as predicted in the article.

rich and underneath it lies a bed of excellent coal. All along that valley stretching from Pittsburgh to Washington will be found, in a very few years, a dense population. Washington itself will be a very inviting place to live. Its beauty of location, its healthfulness, its institutions of learning, and its social attractions are such as to make it a very desirable place to have one's home.

GRAIN AND FRUIT

I paid some attention to both. Never saw the wheat crop better at this time of the year. It promises a very abundant harvest. The fruit is not all killed. In some locations it seems to be safe. It is on the trees yet, and appears to be healthy. The whole country is lovely. The fields are carpeted with green, the trees are putting on their beautiful garments, the flowers are smiling and blushing on hill top, and in valley, and the birds are warbling their bridal songs and building their nests.

AMICUS"

34

Pittsburgh Daily Gazette, Monday, July 3, 1871
"UNIVERSITY EXCURSION [to Chautaugua]

Up the Allegheny Valley. Beautiful and Romantic Scenery.
The Oil Country – Rich Farming Lands.
Chatauqua Lake – Moonlight on the Lake. A Trip Over the
Lake on the Jamestown.
Lake Erie – Resolutions – Homeward Bound.

Editors Gazette –I wrote you last from Parkers' Landing [on the Allegheny River.] We delayed at Scrubgrass twenty minutes for dinner. We reached Oil City at 3 o'clock same day and this being the terminus of the Allegheny Valley Railroad we were transferred without change of cars, to the Oil Creek and Allegheny River Railroad. This part of our journey was of the pleasantest kind. All was expectation and wonder as we passed through the oil country. The derricks protruding themselves on every hillside and valley and the wells in full operation were a novel and interesting sight to the uninitiated.

After Oil City the next place of note was Petroleum Centre, a fine and picturesque country, and celebrated for its oil product. We halted at Shaeffer and Titusville for a short time, where the party received several dispatches from Pittsburgh. The next place of note we reached was Corry, which is a very fine and substantial town. There are many splendid public and private dwellings here. From thence until we reached our destination our way lay through one of the most beautiful and richest sections of country we have ever seen. The land is gently rolling and in a high state of cultivation. Everywhere there is promise of a rich and beautiful harvest.

After one of the pleasantest rides that could possibly have been enjoyed, we reached Mayville, a most beautiful little town on Lake Chautauqua, distant from Pittsburgh 205 miles. It is located in Chautauqua county, which is one of the largest in New York State. It is owing to this fact that it is sometimes called the 'State of Chautauqua.'

We put up at the celebrated and only first class hotel of the place, the Chautauqua Hotel. This is a large and splendid building only lately erected. Two hundred guests can be accommodated here at once. Its internal improvements are first class. Pickerel and bass fish from the lake are always on the table, pure milk, the very best tea and coffee, chicken and a variety of wild game, which are abundant in this region, and all the other substantials and delicacies may be found on the bill of fare; and when you settle your account the charges are found to be little more than the inferior hotels. The house was lately erected and visitors especially, Pittsburghers will be astonished to find how clean and white the bedding is. There are no nocturnal visitors to trouble you such as may be found in many other places of this kind. Here visitors may enjoy themselves as their desire may prompt, <u>ad libitum</u>. There are two pianos for those musically inclined, a billiard ball for the bad boys, and large hall set apart for the display of the 'poetry of motion.' Horace Fox, Esq., is proprietor and presiding genius of the establishment, than whom a more kind hearted, genial and gentlemanly host could not be found any where. To Mr. Fox is due in a very great measure the pleasure and success of the University excursion party. He was assiduous in his attention and administered to their comfort and enjoyment in every conceivable manner. Your correspondent incidentally remarked he had the honor to represent the Pittsburgh GAZETTE, when instantly his hand was extended and the hospitalities of the city extended to him. It was stated to me that the next

146

time he visits the Lake he will be awarded a right royal reception. What the University excursion party think of Horace Fox and of the Chautauqua House will be found embodied in resolutions below.

Had you ever a moonlight ride on the lake? Ain't it grand? Steaming over its placid water in whose pure bosom is reflected all the beauty of heavenly glory – moon and stars and fleecy clouds hidden in its glassy depths. Boating by the 'moonlight on the lake' was the 'order of exercises' after supper. And it was enjoyed as those only can enjoy who have escaped from the din and smoke of the 'Smoky City.' But how much more enjoyable is 'moonlight on the lake' when in company with those who have sweet voices and bright eyes. Such was the privilege enjoyed by those in the boat that had the honor of carrying your correspondent, and this party was the only one honored so.

Next morning a meeting was held of the excursionists to decide the question whether we should proceed as far as Niagara Falls, but the unanimous opinion was that the Chautauqua House was so pleasant, that the Lake so beautiful, and the scenery so surpassingly picturesque, that the party could proceed no further. Accordingly it was agreed upon that the entire party would charter the 'Jamestown,' a steamer that plies on the lake between Mayville and Jamestown, situated at the outlet of the Lake. We embarked on board at 9 o'clock in the morning and made the entire trip to Jamestown and back in four hours. During the trip the expressions of delight, admiration, and astonishment of the party were unbounded.

Chautauqua Lake is situated in Chautauqua county, in the western part of New York State, thirty miles from the Pennsylvania State line. It is one of the principal headwaters of the Allegheny river. It is eighteen miles long by three and a half wide at the widest point. Bemus' Point is the narrowest place, and here the water is sixty feet deep. This lake is pronounced by competent judges to be one of the most beautiful in the world. Professor Rorbacher, who was one of our party, says that it wants only villas and villages to adorn the banks to make it equal to the famous Lake of Ulrich in Switzerland. The lake shore scenery is varied and exceedingly picturesque. The timber of this place is celebrated and the soil rich and productive. Land is worth from sixty to two hundred dollars per acre. The water is the purest of spring water, and Dr. Jillson says it may contain medicinal properties. It is generally as calm and pure as an infant's dream. The lover of the piscatorial art can here find ample scope for his proclivities. The lake abounds in pickerel, bass, and pike. Some have been caught weighing thirty pounds. During our trip we saw plenty of wild fowl, principally wild duck. Turtle in profusion were seen, at which revolvers were used with little effect.

Jamestown is situated at the outlet of the lake. This is a town of some eight thousand inhabitants, and is quite extensively engaged in manufacturing pursuits. It is celebrated for its woolen mills and cabinet manufacturing.

In a snug little villa on the banks of this lake, General McCook, of Ohio fame and family, spent three summers and stated that for health giving properties, it was equal to the most famed summer resorts. Here also Gen. Dunlevy and family seek the sylvan shades and exhilarating breezes, as do many others of lesser note.

There are some snug little villages bordering the lake. One of the principal is De Wittville, where there are some fine country buildings.

At Fairpoint there was a camp meeting, to which we paid a visit, and where some of the party spent the evening.

'Chautauqua' is an Indian name meaning a bag tied in the middle. It received this very appropriate name from the fact that at some parts it is so wide while at others it is so narrow, thus resembling a bag of meal tied in the middle. It is twelve hundred feet above the level of the sea and eight hundred above Lake Erie. From this it will be seen that it is the highest navigable water on this continent with the exception of Lake Depo in the Sierra Navadas [sic].

The only circumstance to mar the happiness of our trip over the lake was that Mr. George Heron of the class of '70 became sea-sick and you may be sure we all heartily pitied him. But Prof. Griggs drew forth from some hidden recess certain mysterious bottles, which Dr. Jillson administered and unalloyed pleasure reigned supreme once more.

Our hearty thanks are due and are hereby tendered to the large hearted and courteous Captain of the splendid steamer Jamestown. T.E. Grandin, Esq., for his great kindness and liberality of charging our party less than one-third fare. Also to his efficient clerk, Mr. S. Manly, and pilot, T.K. Oston. Our thanks are also due to our kind and genial friend, Mr. Williams, who during our trip gave us all desired information. He is the fortunate possessor of over one thousand acres of the richest lake shore lands.

We arrived back at the Chautauqua House at 2 p.m. and found a dinner awaiting us, which was appreciated very much after our lengthened trip.

The afternoon was passed according to the pleasure of the parties. Some went fishing, some sailing, some to the croquet grounds, while several drove to Lake Erie, which is seven miles from Chautauqua. Your correspondent was among the latter. A splendid two-horse carriage having been hired, in company with Messrs. Johns, Roberts, Wood and Stone we stared for this celebrated lake. We drove through the town of Westfield, situated on the border of the lake, which is one of the most beautiful places that could be imagined. Broad, level streets, smooth and solid, bordered with fine shade trees. Don't forget to visit Westfield; it is an exquisitely beautiful spot.

During the evening the musical element of the party was brought into requisition, and the piano gave forth its sweet tones. 'Moonlight on the lake' was again experienced, after which at a late hour the happy gathering were sleeping the sweet sleep of the good and the pure.

We forgot to say that a few of our party proceeded on to Niagara Falls and returned in time to the Chautauqua House to proceed homeward bound with the entire party.

At half-past nine o'clock Saturday morning we bid good-bye to the lovely lake of Chautauqua, its wooded hills and fertile valleys, to the town of Mayville kissed by its balmy breezes, to the Chautauqua House and its large-hearted proprietor, for whom as the cars moved off we gave three rousing cheers.

There is nothing of interest to chronicle of our homeward trip. The weather was delightful and joyous gladness seemed to fill the heart of each one. It was the general cause of comment that the conduct of the students was so exemplary and gentlemanly. This has ever been a cause of remark on former excursions, and this was no exception. True enjoyment can be experienced without the aid of the wine cup.

At a meeting of the members of the excursion party, held in the parlor of the Chautauqua House, the following resolutions were unanimously adopted. . . .

We arrived in Pittsburgh Saturday evening at 9 o'clock. As the party alighted from the cars they assembled together at the Union Depot, and gave three hearty cheers for Col. Wm. Phillips and the Allegheny Valley Railroad.

This ended one of the most pleasant excursions that it has ever been our lot to enjoy. No accident happened to mar the pleasure of the occasion. The weather was all that could have been desired, in short there was a happy combination of circumstances which conduced to add to the pleasure of all.

All honor to Colonel William Phillips, the noble and efficient President of the Allegheny Valley Railroad. Through the GAZETTE the Trustees, Faculty, Alumni and students tender him their hearty thanks. Nor do we forget our good and true friend Wm. Oden Hughart, who was the first to honor in a fitting manner the Western University of Pennsylvania. Who, next year, will initiate the noble example of President Hughart and President Phillips?

We earnestly urge those who have been accustomed to spend the summer at other more fashionable and more expensive summer resorts to try, as an experiment, a few months of the summer here, and we are sure if they will do so that they will not regret their choice. The roads are level and smooth so that driving is a pleasure, and the lake and its attractions excel places where these could not be enjoyed. The Allegheny Valley Railroad is the direct route, and a ride on this sure road in their luxurious palace cars is a pleasure.

W.H.K."

35

Pittsburgh Daily Gazette, Monday July 31, 1871
"WASHINGTON [Again!]

Exhibition of the Fast Horses at the Trotting Park –
Large Attendance – Operations of a 'Three Card Monte'
on the Cars &c.

'There is nothing half so pleasant as riding on a rail,' that is to say, when on board a railway train, seated in a comfortable coach, with all the agreeable surroundings that have marked the brief history of the Chartier's Valley Railroad. This was the experience of the writer, last Friday morning, after he took passage at the Union Depot for the borough of Washington, Pa. One would not, in a year's constant travel, find a pleasanter conductor than Mr. C.W. Paisley, nor more obliging gentlemen than Messrs. L.D. Mathers, baggage master, and Ad. Hall, route agent, on the Washington accommodation. The Friday morning train took out an unusually lively party, most of whom were going to witness the trial of speed between fast trotters and pacers and racers on the course of the Wylie Park Driving Association, about two miles east of Washington. It is not strange, then, that a goodly number of gamblers were on the train, and among the passengers of that ilk was the man who manipulates the three cards for the purpose of winning money from those who are <u>green</u> enough to bet against those 'tricks that are vain.' In other words, the

THE 'THREE CARD MONTE' DEALER

Was there with his little deceptive paste-boards, his 'cappers,' in short, he carried all the implements and possessed just enough of bare-facedness to carry on this little game greatly to the distress of many a greedy chap, who, imagining he had a sure thing of winning the dealer's cash, lost his bottom dollar. With the hope that it may be the means of preventing some of the uninitiated from investing in this deceptive game, we propose to give a brief description of the <u>modus operandi</u> of 'three card monte' for which we are indebted to a veteran 'sport' who accompanied the horse-race party last Friday.

ENTER MONTE DEALER.

No sooner did the train pass the station at Mansfield than the front passenger car was invaded by a countrified looking specimen, attired in a plain suit of Kentucky jeans. His pants were tucked inside of his boot-legs in a negligent manner that would seem to indicate that the fellow had neither ambition nor sense enough to complete his toilet, and the almost idiotic expression of his face was enough to convince any one not particularly observant that the man was not responsible for his uncouth appearance, nor, indeed, for anything that he might say or do, short of cutting a throat or throwing a passenger head long from the train, and even then the feeling towards him would have been one of pity, and the universal expression would doubtless be,

SEND HIM TO DIXMONT

Such a looking thing was the monte dealer. Entering the car, he took an unoccupied seat near the rear end, and, poking his head and half of his body through a window, he commenced talking loudly about an imaginary dog which he described as running a race with the train, with the dog ahead and still increasing his advantage.

'That,' remarked our new found sporting acquaintance, 'is done for the purpose of attracting attention. You will only have to wait a few minutes to see him introduce his game.'

Having thus been posted, we took particular pains to observe all the gambler's movements. In a very short time after he had given a description of the dog and engine race, he drew from his coat pocket three ordinary playing cards. After shuffling them for a minute or two, he related, in a tone of voice loud enough to be heard in all parts of the car, a wonderful story of how he had recently returned from a perilous trip across the plains; starting, he said, from New Mexico on foot, with nothing but a revolver and a pack of cards in his pocket, he was captured by Indians, who tied him up one night and told him he would be tomahawked and scalped next morning at daybreak. With this comfortable intelligence on his mind he turned his attention towards getting away from his captors. In this he succeeded, but in the effort he lost all his cards excepting three, with these three cards he had learned to play a little game, which he would now proceed to show to the gentlemen if they so desired.

HOW THE 'CAPPER' COMES

The three card monte man is always accompanied in his predatory excursions by one or more assistants, who are denominated 'cappers.' These fellows distribute themselves about the car, and as soon as the dealer has finished his Indian story they all gather about him and appear to be watching the three cards with great interest. This is done for the purpose of collecting the green passengers, or 'contributors,' as they are termed by the gamblers. Then the game commences in earnest. The faces of the three cards are shown, one of which is called the winning card. They are then turned face downward, when the dealer remarks that anyone can have the privilege of turning up a card, and that he is willing to bet any amount, from ten to a hundred dollars, that no one can turn the winning card. While the game is at this stage the dealer manages to let the outsiders see that the winning card is plainly marked, and before any of them have made up their minds to invest the 'cappers' pretend to suddenly discover the mark, and commence betting quite lively, winning, of course, every time. This is certain to excite the speculative propensities of the outsiders, who at once 'go down for their pocket books.' By the time they are ready to make their bets the monte man is ready to receive them, having adroitly changed the cards so as to present an unmarked card winning card, with the mark which it had first exhibited transferred to the one of the losing cards. The outsiders make their bets, turn over the wrong card, and is a trice their money is transferred to the pocket of the monte man. In the game last Friday the passengers, or a few of them, rather (for there were many in the train who were content to look on without betting) were fleeced to the extent of about four hundred dollars. Among the victims we observed a couple of hotel keepers who were greedy enough to covet the monte man's money, and who were silly enough to think they had a certainty of winning it. One contributed twenty and the other fifty dollars, whereupon they took back seats and seemed to lose all interest in the game.

It is proper to say that this game was played in the absence of the train officials, otherwise it would not have been permitted.

The game, we think, has been sufficiently described to put the unwary on their guard. It has been practiced all over the country for many years, and it is strange that anybody is caught with it at this late day. The best rule is: 'never bet against any man's game.' Our sporting acquaintance was about right when he remarked 'if a sane man would offer to bet that he could jump four hundred feet in the air, I would be afraid to take him up. If he had not a certainty of winning he would not make such an offer.'

ARRIVED IN WASHINGTON

Aside from the three card swindle, nothing of note occurred during the remainder of the trip to Washington. The passengers employed their time in viewing the largely harvested fields and the growing corn of the fertile valley through which the road passes. At Washington a lively scene was presented. The promised display of fast horses on the race course had brought to the town upwards of two thousand people, mostly from Washington, Fayette, and Greene counties, with a goodly number from Wheeling and from Pittsburgh. Among the noted horse fanciers there assembled we noticed the celebrated Tom Curi, of Carmichael's, Greene county; Colonel John S. Krepps, of Brownsville, Fayette county; Major H.B. Vanvoorhis, of this city, together with many others from various points, all of whom 'talk horses' quite fluently.

THE DRIVING PARK

The track of the Wylie Park Association, as already stated, is situated near the line of the Chartiers Valley Railroad, about two miles this side of Washington. It is circular in form and a half mile in extent, and is on perfectly level ground. As yet it has not been enclosed with a high fence, although it is the intention of the association to do so at an early day. This they feel is necessary to do in order to make the thing pay. It was observed at the races, Friday, that many wealthy individuals who were anxious to witness the exhibition declined to pay the small sum asked for admission, preferring rather to take 'back seats' on the surrounding hills in order to save their 'quarters' and 'halves.' The Association does not think that such people should be entertained for nothing, and they propose, therefore, to shut the course from the vision of all such dead-heads.

THE RACES

Were of a most exciting character. Premiums, amounting to about four hundred dollars, were offered by the Association, and were competed for by twelve or more fast nags. The first contest was a trot by horses that had never made better time than three minutes. The horses entered were as follows: Dr. T.B. Kent entered 'Goldsmith;' Mr. Woodmansic, a bay mare, Isaac Vanvoorhis, a white horse, Tom Collins, a bay mare. The race was mile heats, three in five, and was won by the white horse in three straight heats. Time: 2:54, 2:45, 2:53. None of the other horses made better time than three minutes.

The second contest was between s.b. [sorrel bay?] 'Jeremy,' entered by H.B. Vanvoorhis, and b.m. [bay mare] 'Annie,' entered by Tom Collins. Following is a summary of this trot:

	1st heat	2nd	3rd	4th
Jeremy	2	1	1	1
Annie	1	2	2	2
Time	2:49	2:52	2:52	2:49

'Jeremy' was declared the winner, and was awarded the premium of one hundred dollars.

The next contest was between pacers, with the following entries: Sam'l Barbor entered s.g. [sorrel gray?], 'No Name,' James Seaman, g.g. [gray gelding?], 'Charlie,' James Curti, g.g., 'Post Boy.' This race, like the others, was mile heats, three in five. After the first heat Seamans' horse was withdrawn and the contest was between 'No Name' and 'Post Boy' resulting as follows:

	1st	2nd	3rd	4th	5th
No Name	1	1	2	2	2
Post Boy	2	2	1	1	1

Post Boy taking the last three heats was announced as the victor.

The most exciting contest of the day was that between running horses, the following entries were made: J.F. Reynolds entered s.g. 'Jim Hurley;' Thos. Curl, b.b. [brown bay?], 'Dave;' Maj. Jas. B. Lindsley, b.m., 'Lucy P.; 'Alex Hallam, b.m., 'Fannie;' R. W. Hodgins, s.g., 'Billy Maloy.' Before the racers had gone the first half mile Lindsey's bay mare flew the track and threw her rider, when she was ruled out as a dangerous animal. 'Dave' took the first heat, and seemed to have things pretty much his own way. In the second heat, however, he left the track before he had gone half around and played the same shabby trick in the third, and in the fourth he came in second.

The summary is as follows:

	1st heat	2d	3d	4th
Jim Burley	2	1	1	1
Dave	1	0	0	2
Lucy P	0	0	0	0
Billy Maloy	3	2	2	3
Fannie	4	3	3	4

The race was half mile heats, three in five, and was won, as will be seen, by 'Jim Burley.' The time was not made known.

This exciting sport, we learn, is to be continued at intervals during the season, and will afford an opportunity to our horse men to try the speed and settle of their stock as often as they desire."

36

Pittsburgh Daily Gazette, Tuesday, August 22, 1871
"CHEAT RIVER

Excursion and Fishing Camp.
(Correspondence *Pittsburgh Gazette*)

Editors Gazette: Cheat river correspondence was quite frequent this season, enough to bring the cheating river <u>en vogue</u> for next year's season. I hope that the next generation of fishes will have more numerous families for the benefit of would be fishers of patient proclivities. The fortunes and misfortunes of the Black Fork of cheat river party of Pittsburghers are laid down in the archives of our city to tell the coming generations of the dangers that surrounded their ancestors of heroic renown, permit me to give you a description of the 'Quarry Run' party, which mirrors back the ideal of coming equal rights sociables, and gives us a glimpse into a bright future. Some ladies and gentlemen with superior taste for nature's grandeur in its wild primitive state, resolved to wend their way from the lovely town of Morgantown into the wilderness of the Cheat river to encamp under <u>la etoile's</u> [starry] Canopy. The gentlemen left two days before the ladies, to put up the tents, kitchen, dinner tables, &c. The ladies' tent with rubber cloth cover, comfortable bed and rubber blankets over it; a toilet table with a lovely bouquet of lobelias and wild lilies, an arm chair all fashioned by the male members of the party; the gentlemen's tent covered with the glorious stars and stripes, gave one the idea that under such a protective Union, no wolf nor bear, nor panther, under the form of a wild cat should ever be dangerous, at the same time, it is refreshing in our over cultivated, over progressive times, to see ladies and gentlemen prohibit the kid glove of fashionable society and enjoy nature in her own purity and beauty, to laugh at rain and storm, like Nimrods and Dinas, and throw overboard the affected sensitivities and ridicule of the parlor to be once more natural and true to their better nature. The ladies followed with the provisions and, gentle reader, mind, provisions prepared by their own hands, they reached 'Quarry Run' under the matronship of an accomplished lady, Miss D., and established themselves with the help of the gentlemen so comfortably that this, combined with the beauty of the scenery, inspired Miss D., who gave the name of 'Camp Eden' to the lovely spot. You ask what is 'Quarry Run?' An oasis in the wilderness of Cheat River. Alpine Lilies raise their crests far toward heaven shutting out from the world a beautiful little plateau where the tents were built. Placidly, limpid and calm flows black hued Cheat past the camp to break, a hundred yards higher, its angry, roaring waves against massive rocks, amongst which 'Squirrel rock' of immense dimension and about fifty feet high reigns supreme and makes the water boil as in a witches kettle. The selection of the camp was certainly well made. Camp regulations were strict. The matron was supreme, all had to yield obedience and did it cheerfully. No lady to be out of camp without permission, and after dark no lady and gentleman under any circumstance were permitted to be out together. A forgetful couple was called to come in immediately, and the summons created merriment for the balance. The scenery was beautiful – nothing can speak more or better of the supremacy of God. Such surroundings lift the heart far above the groveling nature of man, make us forget sorrow and pain, even in the existence of passions, we draw nearer the highest in His rich bountiful love, we forget the shortcomings of our earthly pilgrimage. A drive of four hours through the hills and dales – very conducive to the health, and it gives a wonderful circulation to the blood – brings the traveler from Morgantown, West Va., to Ice's Ferry; this past, rise the ruins and buried hopes of friend K's iron mills and oil wells. . . . From there to Leg's Mill a rocky path leads to the camp. Little pebbles, from about the size of an egg to that of a feather bed, lend a certain elasticity to the steps, which raises the mind far above the common level of life's hidden path. Unmistakably real pebbles of antiquity, moss and ferns, lobelias, wild lilies and convolvuluses to beautify and soften, the trees covered with parasites and climbing plants, form alternately with the sky a canopy over the head. Then comes a bend and the pebbles change into rocks, a little run forming a natural basin, the cool rocks formed the pantry of the lady fishers' a bridge of rocks and at a little distance the green shady plateau 'Quarry Run.' I am thinking of a new era is dawning, to see such noble looking specimens of the so-called strong sex bound by the slivery chords of friendship, uniting with their congenial sisters to enjoy the pure air, the fresh enlivening powers of nature in her primitive state. The ladies partaking, under the safeguard of a kind friend, in the sports of the gentlemen on the rocks, river and mountains alike, is certainly indicative of a change in the existing spheres of the sexes. The gentlemen look martial in their high boots and fishing costumes, two of them were the cooks, two their assistants, two set the table, and the ladies you ask? A long dinner table was over shadowed by shady trees, daily a beautiful bouquet of wild flowers and ferns graced the centre of the table, the dishes even were ornamented with ferns and leaves, the table laden fishes, roasted chicken, fruits, and cakes to tempt an epicure, a scene from Olymph, nothing disturbed the harmony of this Walhalla but a requiem sung by a young lady over her lost or missing pocket handkerchief. I am not saying too much by asserting that I had not enjoyed anything so much for years past. . . ."

37

Pittsburgh Daily Gazette, September 12, 1872
"CASTLE SHANNON

Progress of the Work on the Narrow Gauge –
Subdivision of the Company's Land – The Immense Coal
Trade on the Road, Etc.

The great enterprise which is to bring into close and direct communication with the city one of the most beautiful, picturesque and fertile of our outlying districts rapidly approaches completion. That Passenger trains will be running between Pittsburgh and Castle Shannon within six weeks at the furthest, is a fixed fact, as far as lies in the power of any human agency. During the past few months the work has been rapidly pushed forward, and its progress has fully met the sanguine expectations of those most interested in its speedy conclusion.

On Monday last the President and Directors of the company inspected the work, going over the entire length of the road, and expressed themselves so highly gratified with its satisfactory progress and the sure indication of its early completion. The grading is almost finished to Castle Shannon; the greater portion of the road is ready for the cross-ties, and the iron has been laid, and the road ballasted and placed in complete running order for a considerable distance beyond the bridge crossing Knox's Hollow, about three miles from the city. The first bridge (the one referred to) is already completed, and at the time mentioned, a trial of it was made with the most satisfactory results. A heavy locomotive doing duty upon the road was run over the bridge quite rapidly, two or three times, without causing any perceptive swaying. It is well built and strong, the heaviest timbers entering into its construction, and of its durability there can be no question. A fifty-ton locomotive might pass over it with as little danger as the light locomotive required for the narrow gauge. It was built by Mr. George W. Bitner, and is truly a model bridge, and will bear favorable comparisons with those upon any railroad in the country.

The remaining bridges, which are fast being finished, will be equally secure and thoroughly complete in their construction. The road bed, nearly the whole length of the road, is of solid rock, and the grade is all that could be desired. It is the intention to ballast it with stone, thus rendering it as solid and substantial as it can possibly be made.

One thing that was particularly perceptible to the party during their visit, and equally gratifying, consisted in the remarkable ease with which the road has been graded, a comparatively small amount of cutting and no tunneling having been required. After crossing the ravines over which the bridges are constructed, the road follows the valley the entire distance to Castle Shannon. Owing to the facility with which the road has been graded, the estimated cost of building it has been considerably reduced, and we cannot but congratulate the company upon their good fortune in having secured the services of so competent an engineer for the building of the road as R. C. Patterson, Esq., who has had the work in charge. To the indomitable energy and untiring devotion to their interests of the President, Milton D. Hays, Esq., who has from the out start given the work of construction his personal supervision, the company also owes much. Mr. Hayes, although a comparatively young man, is possessed of the ability, judgment, foresight and prudence for the management of an enterprise from which so much is justly expected. The force of workmen employed upon the construction of the road is large, and the company have advertised for additional men to complete the grading and to lay cross ties. It is the intention of the company, and present appearances favor their plans, to have passenger trains running between Pittsburgh and Castle Shannon by the middle of next month at the latest.

The road will be equipped in the best manner throughout, and the passenger cars are designed to afford passengers the same comfort and conveniences they experience in traveling upon the best regulated roads. The contract for these cars has been given out, and it is confidently expected that they will be ready by the time the road is completed. Three locomotives are now in use upon the road, a fourth is in the shops, and another is being made to order by the firm of Porter, Bell & Co. One of the engines now doing service is similar in appearance and construction to the locomotives used on broad gauge railways, and is a beautiful piece of workmanship. It was manufactured for the Company by the Pittsburgh Locomotive Works, and was put upon the road a few weeks ago. The Company have on the road a large number of coal cars which are all brought into constant requisition in conveying coal for their mines to supply their extensive trade demand.

Some idea of the immense amount of coal mined and sold by the company may be obtained from the fact that from twenty-five to thirty trains of 22 cars each, freighted with 'black diamonds,' daily pass over their road from their mines to the incline, whence it is conveyed by means of the latter to their depot on Carson street, above the Monongahela suspension bridge. From three to five hundred teams are loaded daily, and it quite frequently happens that the quantity mined is inadequate to meet the supply. If any of our readers are possessed of a desire to see a sight of unusual activity, let them repair to the coal depot of the Pittsburgh and Castle Shannon Railroad, in South Pittsburgh, at any time during the day, and witness the operation of loading the score or two of wagons that may always be found in waiting. This work is unceasingly going on from an early hour in the morning till night, and double the amount would be done were the company possessed of the facilities for filling all orders that might be easily obtained. A considerable portion of their heavy coal trade come from the South Side rolling mills, whose heavy wagons may at all times be seen about the depot. In the mills alone ten thousand bushels of coal are daily consumed, and so rapidly is it burned that the coal taken from the mines in the morning is all in ashes by six o'clock in the evening. The railroad, when completed to its proposed termination at Finleyville, Washington county, will open a tract of coal lands seventeen miles in extent, upon which no operations have yet been made. Surely the coal trade of the company will alone pay for the building of the road.

But a more important consideration even than the immense coal fields traversed by the road is the delightful prospect presented to our citizens for procuring suburban homes in one of the richest, most beautiful and inviting regions upon which the eye of man ever rested. Too much cannot be said of the lovely country reached by this road, and yet it must be seen to be fully appreciated. The pure air, fresh water, delightful scenery, productive soil, and comparatively even surface of the lands owned by the company of Castle Shannon, render them most attractive and desirable as sites for beautiful country residences. Three hundred acres of these lands have been sub-divided into lots ranging from one quarter to three acres in size, upon which the proposed village of Castle Shannon is to be built.

While the lots are large, being of suitable dimensions for country residences, the streets are of sufficient width – sixty feet. A number of acres have been reserved in the most eligible portion of the tract for a public park, which may one day become the chief attraction of the place, and the fact should be borne in mind, by all who attend the forthcoming sale of the property. The plans have been prepared, and may be seen at the office of the Company, No. 75, Fourth avenue, or at the station on Carson street, South Pittsburgh. We are unable at present to announce the date of sale, but presume it will take place about the time the road is completed, or in a month or so hence. None who contemplate the purchase of a suitable lot for a suburban home should fail to acquaint themselves with the location and surroundings of this property, and learn fully concerning the advantage and accessibility in the meantime and make their arrangements to attend the sale whenever it may come off.

While desirable sites for country residences between the rivers and on the North Side are held at exorbitant figures, yet in this great and almost unexplored South Side region lying contiguous to the city, they can be had on reasonable terms. When again we take into consideration the fact that trains will be run on the railroad, which is to bring this section into close communication with the city every twenty or thirty minutes during the day and evening, and that Castle Shannon may be reached at about the same rate of fare as is charged for riding an equal distance on other railroads will be made manifest, the reason why the approaching sale should be largely attended. The term on which the lots will be sold will be sufficiently easy to enable all purchasers to meet their payments.

As will be recollected by our readers, a subdivision of lots on the line of the Pittsburgh and Castle Shannon Railroad, called the Fair Haven plan, was sold at auction in the month of May. Upon these lots from fifteen to twenty homes are now in process of erection, and work on many will soon be commenced. The present prospects of Fair Haven are most flattering indeed, and it will doubtless soon become a flourishing village. New buildings are also going up elsewhere on the line of the road most surely indicating that, as soon as it is fully in operation, property along its line will materially enhance in value. From what we saw, during an excursion to Castle Shannon of the property and the railroad, we are confidently of the opinion that the road will be one of the principal outlets for our densely crowded population, and that Castle Shannon will eventually become one of our most populous suburban towns. Of the date upon which the great sale of lots will take place, due announcement will be made."

— 38 —

Pittsburgh Daily Gazette, January 30, 1873
"CORREPONDENCE
CHEAT RIVER VALLEY

The Immense Timber Regions – View of
Surpassing Grandeur – The Pittsburgh, Virginia and
Charleston Railroad. [See f/n 1, p. 175]
(Correspondence of the *Pittsburgh Gazette.)*

Pittsburgh, from her very favorable location, extensive manufactures, and excellent transportation facilities, coupled with an untiring energy and the American go-a-headativeness, has built her wealth to colossal proportions, and now grasping for new materials, new avenues to wealth, stretches her influence in all directions, down the valley of the Ohio, up both the Allegheny and Monongahela, and into

PITTSBURGH IN 1874: From Brownsville Avenue and Gray Road, now William Street.
Source: *Fleming's Views of Old Pittsburgh.*

all their tributaries, and not least among the latter we call attention to Cheat River which, one hundred miles south from Pittsburgh up to the Monongahela, empties into it. [It's actually 89.6 miles.]

On the point of land between the two rivers is the pleasant, beautiful little town of Point Marion, which only awaits the completion of the extension of the Monongahela Slackwater [Navigation Company], and the Pittsburgh, Virginia and Charleston R.R. to start it into busy life. It is favorably located for a manufacturing town, as the hills in the immediate vicinity are full of excellent lime stone, and coking coal. Here A. D. Frankenberry and Co. have an excellent Steam Circular Saw Mill, and are doing a good trade in the timber and lumber business, and each year saw considerable of the lumber used by the glass manufactures of Pittsburgh in flattening glass.

For a number of years much of the timber used in building the finest steamers afloat on western waters has been cut on the Monongahela and floated down it to a market, but the supply is now well nigh exhausted and other sources must be looked to supply the vast demand. And we know of no other source to supply the great demand than up among the hills of Cheat Mountains. And as all men in the vast coal trade, steamboat builders, railroad men, and indeed nearly all of the citizens of your city, are deeply interested in all that pertains to its future welfare, I propose to give a few items in relation to the future prospects of the timber trade of Cheat river.

From the mouth Cheat up to Pridevale [Pricedale?] is ten miles. Here Chase, Smyth & Co. of Pittsburgh, have an iron works (not now in operation) and a large tract of land, one and a half miles above is Lye's Steam Saw Mill. One year ago this was the head of navigation, as but very few flat boats ever ascended above, and but few rafts of timber were ever run out above this. But in the fall of 1871, A. D. Frankenberry and Co., C. Lye, Sadler & Dilliner Brothers, and others by heavy blasting, blew down the great rocks in the channel and removed the difficulties and dangers of running rafts and boats from the Beaver Hole four and a half miles above Lye's Hill. Since then on a small rise in the river a very large quantity of timber has been floated in rafts from Beaver Hole and with but slight loss and little danger. This improvement cost the parties $193.00, and has been of immense benefit to parties owning timber and timber lands.

Between Lye's Mill and the Beaver Hole persons loving the stupendous grandeur and sublimity of Nature's works will find many objects of vast interest. Among the most prominent I may mention the Squirrel Rock, an immense solid rock standing in the middle of the river, and rising about thirty-five feet above low water mark, its sides so steep that no person has ever been known to climb to the top, and yet on the top of the rock lies a stretch of timber, showing that at some distant day in the past Cheat river was so high as to float it there.

About one mile up the river from the Squirrel Rock we go up the steep mountain side to an object of great interest, viz: The Panther Rock, which stands on one of the highest points of Cheat Mountain. Between the rock and the main hill is a chasm about fifteen feet wide and many feet deep, and until recently it was considered impossible to reach the rock except by a bridge, but now a way is known by which a man may gain its top from below.

The view from the top is one of surpassing grandeur. Almost directly under your feet yet thousands of feet below, rolls the deep, dark waters of the famous Cheat, winding its serpentine course along, sparkling in the sunlight. We have seen scenes of the great places of resort, Lookout [Mountain near Chattanooga], towering above the clouds, Kenesaw [Mountain, Ga.], 'dark in its glory,' Sacser's Head in South Carolina, but none of them compare to the views from here in extent of vision, in splendor, in grandeur, in sublimity. Near by is 'Creeper Rock,' once the 'home' and 'copper shop' of a man, who made cedar baskets. Below this and apparently hanging to the mountain side, is the 'Haystack Rock.' It surely stands on a sandy foundation. How large this monster is we cannot say, but not less than one hundred feet long, 60 feet wide, and one hundred feet high. It looks as if its foundation is giving way under the immense weight; and at any moment might go thundering to the river below.

We might mention also White Oak Falls, Grassy Island, White Hole, etc., and we are at the Beaver Hole, which is the largest eddy on the river, and an excellent harbor for rafts, boats, etc. etc. Here Stents, Keyser & Co. own a large tract of timber land. (Indeed we are just now up to the timber.) They have a number of hands and teams getting out cross-ties for the P.V. & C. R.R. They have made a number of 'pikes' which from the heads of their three logways reach out in all directions to their timber. Nearly all the timber cut here is now rafted and run out. Here Butcher and Bro. have rafted a lot of as good steamboat timber as ever floated. At the lower end of Beaver Hole is an excellent fish pot, out of which a great many fine fish have been taken. Here lives Henry Rohr, whose dwelling is the last we will see for many miles along the river. Near here, on the west side, is the famous Cheat view, which is yearly visited by scores of visitors, who travel miles to see its grandeur. On the east side are the Raven Rocks, whose brown heads, lifting themselves high above all other surrounding objects, have for ages battled with the Storm King, and bid defiance to his blasts.

To Bee Run from Beaver Hole is one mile. Here are two logways (places down the side of the mountain prepared in which to either roll or slide timber) a vast mount of timber of the best oak, poplar and chestnut. One half mile above is another tract. Sentz, Keyser & Co.'s land, covered with excellent oak, and one and one half miles above is the Devil's Den, a rough rocky place in the river, and has an appropriate name, but it is said by river men that the 'Old Boy' is not often seen about. Here is Sadler & Ruble's logway, and back of it is a tract of timber land not excelled in quality or quantity in the mountains. At three and a half miles we are at the mouth of Sandy Creek, a rough, wild mountain stream, coming in on the east side, and often rising high enough to make a rafting freshet in Cheat. Here Mr. Hagans has a large tract of timber land and plenty of as fine oak as grows, and besides others, whose names I do not now recall, own large tracts of timber land.

We are now nineteen and one fourth mile from the mouth, and at three miles more we are at Ben McMullen's logway. Here G. T. Dilliner and A. D. Frankenberry & Co. own one of the best tracts of timber land along the river. The land is covered with the finest lot of white oak, yellow popular, chestnut and yellow locust, and a part of the land is of an excellent quality.

Near here a Mr. Snebble is getting out a large quantity of railroad cross-ties for the P.V. & C. R.R. and three miles above is Sadler and Dilliner's logway, all these are on the west side of the river and on the east side Mr. G. M. Hagans, of Morgantown, West Virginia, owns a tract of one thousand acres, and an immense lot of fine timber, all of which is for sale on very favorable terms.

Nine and a half miles above the Beaver Hole is Cheat River Falls, a smooth rock extending entirely across the river. One half mile above the falls, is Rude's logway, in the close vicinity of which are large tracts of timber land, and two and a half miles from the Falls is Sadler and Dilliner Bros. No. '76' timber lately bought of Dr. Ambler. Here for miles the eye sees only timber, and 'timber that is timber,' poplar, hemlock, and chestnut in endless quantities and the best that grows. Sadler and Dilliners have cut an immense lot of saw logs and each log bears their mark, the peculiar X known along the river. Two miles above is the Green Hale, and we are through Cheat Mountain two miles above is Albrightville, the first civilization since we left the Beaver Hole, except the 'homes' of the timber men; fourteen miles above Albrightville is Rowlesburg, where the B. & O. R.R. crosses Cheat, and we are about six miles and a half from the mouth.

From Beaver Hole to Rowlesburg is the place where the timber grows, and to which we call attention. We have only guessed at a few points, where a few of the bold pioneers are at work. Both sides of the river, every run, ravine, nook and corner, is full of heavy growth of timber, which awaits only the woodman's axe impelled by the energy of capital, and the logs may be floated to a profitable market.

It is expected that an effort will be made during this session of Congress for aid to assist in clearing out a channel in Cheat to the better float timber to a market.

But now is the time to purchase. We cannot close this important sketch without an allusion to John G. Sadler, one of the old pioneers of Cheat river, and who is well acquainted with all the timber lands, and who will be glad to render aid to all who wish to invest, if they call upon him."

ᐁ

— 39 —
Pittsburgh Daily Post, November 13, 1874
"BELLE VERNON, PA.

A Chatty and Interesting Correspondent –
Bound to Have His Say –
A Progressive and Thriving Village.

(Cor[respondent]. of *The Post*)

Belle Vernon, Pa., Nov. 11, 1874

Thinking that perhaps a little scribble from one up the Monongahela river might do to fill in some corner of your valuable paper, I write you.

We occasionally see that some one or more furnish matter from this region for the other papers of your city, and some might judge from these articles appearing only in the *Commercial* and *Telegraph,* that we of the uncertified school had nothing to say, or did not know how to say it, or rather – which is most likely – had no right to say anything. Now, the first supposition is incorrect as this fully attests, and the second is like unto it only that we cannot wield the pen of some of the *Telegraph*'s correspondents – sorry indeed – and the third, thank the Lord, is of the past, and marks one of the darkest pages of American history. Yet we must say, we had our say at all times, only, we think, because we would have it, come what might.

Our village of twelve hundred inhabitants is three miles above Lock number four, right on the line between Westmoreland county and ours – Fayette – and we will wager a big apple there is not a town on the Monongahela has more thrift and business, and handles more money than we do.

Messrs. R. C. Schmertz & Co.'s far-famed two glass manufactories are situated here, employing about one hundred and fifty men, and any one knows that the wages glass operatives receive is no small item itself. Then the great and world widely known distillery of Messrs. John Gibson's Son & Co. is just on the outskirts of the town. Now we see some great big moral idea persons hold up their hands in holy horror at us being so closely situated to a distillery. Just keep cool a minute until we tell you how that mammoth concern, employing sixty or seventy men, is managed. But we cannot go into detail, yet can say for the quiet of your minds, the whisky made there is under the supervision of members of church, and strictly sober. Not one ounce of it is sold, given away or used about the establishment of our town either. Then we have a foundry here, Johnston & Mackey making stoves, grates, &c. A boat yard and lumber mill run by L. M. & W. F. Speer; also coal works just at the upper end of the town, employing eighty to ninety men, owned by the same firm. We have also an extensive lumber mill, run by Johnson & Anderson, who make and furnish boxes for the glass factory. Messrs. Hunt & McClain have a very fine flouring mill here too.

We have twenty-two stores and shops in our town, and business for all. And yet we have no licensed house for selling liquors; but have two good hotels. We have tin shops, jewelry store, shoe shops, merchant tailors, marble shop, blacksmith shops, almost everything. So you see this is some place.

We have a steam boat, making two trips a day between this place and Brownsville, twelve miles above us.

We are directly on the line of the connecting link between the Pittsburgh and Connellsville Railroad and the old Hempfield Railroad at Washington. This link we are satisfied will be made before long, as there has been thousands of dollars already expended just across the river from our place and at other points in Washington county.[1]

To be sure there is a temporary suspension of this work for the present, yet there can be no good reason given for an abandonment, and from all we can learn the work will resume soon.

This link is one of the important items making up the sagacity, foresightedness and thrift of the Baltimore and Ohio Railroad, whilst it adds incalculable value and benefits to our town.

But suppose we are tedious, so will close. Yet, if we see this in *The Post*, will write again; if not, 'O.K.'

Yours Respectfully, Selkirk."

∾

---

[1]The Pittsburgh, Virginia and Charleston RR completed its line up the Monongahela (Mile 32) in 1873. There were delays; it, finally, reached W. Brownsville (opposite Brownsville at Mile 56) in 1881.

Pittsburgh Daily Post, December 12, 1878
"THE HIGH WATERS

The Booming Rivers and Prostrated
Telegraph Lines

The Railroads all Right-Damage
Along the Allegheny

Considerable damage resulted yesterday from the high water, and as the rivers still kept rising till a late hour last night, much uneasiness was felt for to-day. At 2 o'clock the rivers were on a stand at this point and as they had been falling for several hours at points further up stream it may safely be said the worst is past. The railroads are in good working order again but the telegraph wires are down in many places. Following are the particulars:

THE MONONGAHELA

The Monongahela showed twenty-four feet and some inches at eleven o'clock last night and was still rising a little. There was no driftwood floating. The depth at the Smithfield street bridge was maintained principally by the raging torrents from the Allegheny, which forced the water back into the Monongahela. The lower dam [at Mile 2] was not visible; indeed there was scarcely a riffle in the river to show where the dam is located. The Clinton Iron mills and the mill of Dilworth, Porter & Co., were the only two on the South Side which were compelled to suspend operations in consequence of the high water. The upper river packets made their trips yesterday, but no boats went down stream from this point. Work was suspended at different coal pits along the Monongahela.

The coffer dam at Davis Island was completely submerged and a temporary frame building erected there was carried away. This will be but a trifling loss, however. The coffer dam had withstood the current according to latest accounts, but just what damage has been done to it cannot be told till the waters recede.[1]

HIGH WATER RECORD

Twenty-four feet and a half is pretty deep water but the Monongahela has reached that stage frequently before, as is shown in the following table giving the high water records of that stream:

	[Ft.]	[In.]
November 10, 1810	32	--
February 10, 1832	35	--
February 1, 1840	29[?]	9
April 19, 1852	31	7[?]
April 12, 1860	29	7
September 29, 1861	30	9½
January 20, 1862	28	7
April 22, 1862	25	--
March 4, 1865	24	--
March 18, 1865	31	4
April 1, 1865	21	6
May 12, 1865	21	6
December 14, 1873	25	6
January 8, 1874	22	4
December 28, 1875	21	6
September 19, 1876	23	--
January 17, 1877	27	7

---

[1]The Davis Island Lock and Dam was being built at Avalon (Mile 5) on the Ohio River. Completed in 1885, it established Pittsburgh's harbor which also required the removal of L&D #1 at Mile 1.1 on the Monongahela River.

PITTSBURGH SIDE OF THE ALLEGHENY

There was not a great deal of damage on the Pittsburgh side of the Allegheny. The water at midnight was within a few feet of the Duquesne way sidewalk. The cellars of the Robinson House and of Rhodes brewery, as well of several other houses on Duquesne way were flooded. The proprietors anticipated this event, however, and were prepared for it. The water was backed up in the sewers until the cellars of different establishments on Penn avenue and Liberty street were also flooded. Among these were the cellars of Joseph Horne & Co.'s retail store, under Library Hall, and of Marvin's cracker bakery on Liberty street. The latter firm was compelled to remove two thousand barrels of flour from their cellar to the floor above.

The chief damage on this side of the Allegheny was confined to the old water works. The foundation on the western side of the old Cooper engine house was washed away by the high waters some days ago, and yesterday more earth caved in, while some of the studding which the workmen had gotten in place to hold up the structure was also washed out. The water last evening completely covered the two Cooper engines to the depth of seven feet. It was also washing about the foundation of the boiler house located nearest the river, and the workmen were fearful last night that this foundation, too, would give away, and the battery of boilers be wrecked. The steam pipes which connect the other two batteries were disconnected from that in jeopardy last evening, so that the pipes would not be lost if the boiler house did fall. No damage was done to the old Hercules and Samson engines which are still at work, so that no inconvenience will be suffered from a limited supply of water in the reservoir.

THE NORTH SIDE

Shortly after ten o'clock yesterday morning the pier marks on the Suspension bridge showed twenty-one feet of water. At six o'clock in the evening it had risen three feet more, and at midnight the marks indicated twenty-five feet, and rising at the rate of one or two inches an hour. All day and night the water has been flowing swift, bringing with it considerable driftwood. The Penn cotton mill, near the Suspension bridge, was obliged to stop operations on account of the pit filling with water, and the Eagle mill, not far distant, did likewise, the water backing up the sewer. Bradley's woolen mill was almost submerged. At the Exposition building the water has reached the first floor and the structure is entirely surrounded by water. Further down the river many cellars are flooded. Above the Ft. Wayne railroad bridge for quite a distance the cellars of many of the inhabitants on River avenue are submerged and some of them have removed their household goods to the upper stories. At Koff & Voegtley's lumber yard and saw-mill the water has surrounded the mill, the water reaching Main street, some distance in the rear. Operations of course have been stopped as the mill can only be reached by skiffs. All the machinery in that lower part of the Standard Manufacturing Company's building was removed in order to save it from damage by the water, which soon took its place. McFadden street is covered with water for some distance from the river, the depth of the water a some places being nearly four feet. Herr's Island is almost hidden from view. The new paint works building at Willow Grove station, on the West Penn railroad, is cut off from the land by water. The water has reached the bridge at Pine Creek. Thus far the West Penn and Ft. Wayne Railroads have suffered no damage by the flood and all the trains have been about on time.

THE RAILROADS

The railroads suffered most severely from the snow and wind on Tuesday, and the damage has now generally been repaired. Beyond a few delays no inconvenience was suffered by the roads running westward from this city. The Pennsylvania Railroad seems to have suffered most.

Telegraph poles and trees were blown across the track, and yesterday freight engine No. 296 ran into obstructions on the tracks near Conemaugh furnace. Two other engines ran off the track between here and Johnstown. All of these were slight accidents however, and though yesterday morning's trains were behind time all trains came in on time yesterday. Indeed the trains on all the roads, centering at the Union Depot, were on time. There was some danger of the Pittsburgh & Erie and Cleveland & Pittsburgh roads being submerged, but the trains all left on time. The trestle work of the new Lake Erie road near the Smithfield street bridge was submerged, but the piles have withstood the current. The mangers of the new line say the greatest inconvenience to them results from the loss of time, as the contractors cannot proceed with the work so long as the waters remain at their present stage. The Connellsville road, West Penn and the Charleston & Virginia escaped serious damage. On the Connellsville line the trains were delayed in the morning by the snow. There was a tremendous fall of snow in the mountains in Fayette county and all along the Connellsville line.

THE TELEGRAPH LINES

The telegraph wires and in some places telegraph poles were broken down by the weight of the snow along this line and the chief delay was occasioned by the fact that trainmen were bound to run on printed schedule; telegraph orders could not be had. This waiting of one train on another caused much delay. Trains are running all right now however. The telegraph lines along the Pennsylvania and other railroads were also broken in many places, and the Western Union wires too were pulled down. There was but little interruption to communication with western points. The greatest damage resulted with the lines running East and South. Last night the Western Union wires running to western points were in good working order. The situation was quite different with the eastern wires. The wires on the Pennsylvania road were still down between Sang Hollow and Conemaugh at two o'clock this morning. It was expected, however, that they would be in place in time for daylight business this morning, which will then give the Western Union Company all they need for eastern business. The other eastern or 'pike' route of the Western Union Company is partly disabled this side of West Newton. The telegraphers had but two eastern wires last night for the transaction of business, one running to Philadelphia and the other to Baltimore. The usual complement for the eastern business is twenty-three wires. The difficulties of the telegraphers may therefore be imagined when we state that full press reports were sent from Washington, New York, and other points to this city, whence the news was transmitted to further western cities."

&

— 41 —

Monongahela Daily Republican, July 15, 1880
"UP THE [Monongahela] RIVER

A Delightful Trip and Where To Take It

Now that the hot weather has set in so persistently, people are looking to see how they can enjoy a few cool breezes without any trouble. Pittsburghers naturally look to the Monongahela, on whose sweeping surface fresh air can always be found. Walking its sultry streets, roasting in heated rooms, or worn out with toil in its busiest marts, the denizen of the Smoky City has only to turn his face up this valley, and within half an hour his eye will be feasting itself on the most beautiful panorama of hill and meadow, while his heated face will be cooled by an ever present breeze delicately perfumed with bloom of elder or rich with the odor of newly cut clover. The passenger steamers of the Monongahela Packet Line afford every opportunity to the pleasure seeker, the invalid, or the exhausted business man to get away from the sultry city for a little while. The rates are only nominal, and family parties are carried very cheap.

The afternoon boats are best for those who wish to go to headwaters; leaving at 4 o'clock, just in time to enjoy the evening cool, and see the shadows of the hills mirrored in the river. The pleasure-seeker takes a chair on the forward deck; no dust, no smoke, no cinders: no cramped up car seat, no dashing past unseen rural beauties, no jolting of brake, nor rattle of car wheel. Only to sit and be cool, while the majesty of the river scenery breaks into view at each turn of the winding stream, growing nearer and expanding into foreground, then fading slowly away into the mists that are outlined against the column of smoke rising into the sky from the unlidded hell of Pittsburgh's fire and furnace.[1]

Small towns, with jutting levee, are touched, bags and barrels and bales rolled off, passengers exchanged, forming a sort of between-the-scenes rest; the bell rings as if to lift the curtain, and the unfolding of another section of the panorama begins. These towns have their history—are the outlying tributaries to Pittsburgh's business, and interesting to those whose knowledge of them has heretofore been confined to endorsing the name on a business envelope. There is beautiful BRADDOCK, known and read of all men, and this too is the anniversary month of her famous battle; there is McKEESPORT whose pipe works and sheet iron mills are hives of honest industry, and whose people consume 700 cags [kegs?] of beer per day; on the hill yonder we see the engineers leveling for a railroad bridge over which the Lake Erie road is to cross, and thence up the north bank of the Yough. Here is ELIZABETH, the old town with its solid people and its handsome girls; here is MONONGAHELA CITY, the metropolis of the valley, a little city of homes; its streets avenues of shade trees; the center of the coal trade, the shipping point of Washington county's great wool trade. Here is BELLEVERNON, with its two Pittsburg industries in the shape of glass works, and a Philadelphia enterprise in the Gibsonton Distillery, the largest and most complete in the State, and where is made the Monongahela Cabinet Whisky (said to be so good in case of sickness) and known the world

---

[1]The Pittsburgh Brownsville and Geneva Packet Company operated three steamboats in 1880. All were built in W. Brownsville/ Brownsville. The 284-ton *GENEVA*, built in 1871, ran on the Mon for 14 years. Built in 1878, the 163-ton *GERMANIA* ran for an incredible 20 years. The *JOHN SNOWDON*, 302 tons, ran from 1876-1887.

over. This is FAYETTE CITY with its glass works, its brass band, lots of happy people and entirely too many Democrats. Now we are passing through the Water Gap, a lovely stretch, which is not surpassed in picturesque beauty by any scene on any river. Next comes CALIFORNIA, whose fine college is the pride of the valley, and an honor to the State. The people here have one love, that is for their college, they have one devotion, that is, for the welfare of the students, they have one pride, that is in the home life of her people. Its streets are horribly dusty in summer, and wretchedly muddy in winter, yet every girl can play the harpsichord, and every boy reads the first page of [Julius] Caesar['s *Gallic Wars*], which divides . . . Gaul [France] into *tres partes* as readily as he can bat a ball. Then the steamer swings into BROWNS-VILLE, a solid old town where the people are mostly aristo-cratic and rich, a town just awakening from a ten years sleep, but which when roused by the New Life will step at once into that activity and prominence which its employed capital will certainly bring about.

Here the passenger goes to sleep; over the transom comes in the coolest of breezes, and before long he tucks the blankets about him, and dreams that he is resting on a bank of wild violets, while some angel sent by Morpheus[2] fans him with the full sweep of her silver feathered wing. He is not disturbed by fear of fire, for in each berth hangs life preserv-ers, on each deck is a sleepless watchman, by each gang-way are buckets kept constantly filled with water, and beside two powerful force pumps are the carefully coiled fire-hose, *always attached* and ready to deluge the first spark that may happen to show its wicked eye. More perfect protection could hardly be vouchsafed. While we sleep the boat plows its way into the upper Monongahela, and when we awake the

---

[2]In classical mythology, the goddess of dream.

head of navigation has been reached. The bell announces breakfast, and with a sharpened appetite, unknown in the heated city, one goes to the table, and amid the perfume of coffee with real cream, berries with mountain dew on them, and tomatoes whose blush is deepened by the garnish of pounded ice, the passenger thinks of the six foolish friends who took 'some other route' or stayed at home to risk idiocy or incineration under the sulphurous heat-clouds that envelope dear old Pittsburg. Seeking the pilot house, the tourist finds an intelligent and courteous wheel-man who points out new beauties and fresh delights as the boat swims over the ripples of the loveliest river in America.

The day is before us, much to amuse, lots of room to promenade, plenty of companionable society, obliging captains who think it no trouble to make you comfortable, attentive clerks, careful engine-men, and polite servants. A book or paper, a segar, a snooze in the clean state room, a good dinner, a siesta, a look at the glorious sunset, a cup of tea, and then home again – refreshed, re-invigorated, rested. It is all so easy, so comfortable and withal so cheap that he who knows of this water-way to a day's recreation, and does not yield to its seduction is careless of his health, and too blind to see the beckoning of Hygeia[3] as she points her finger up the Monongahela – the Islandless river — the home of Zephyr,[4] and the inviting art gallery where nature has lavished her richest colors and painted her most beautiful landscapes."[5]

೭

---

[3]The ancient Greek goddess of health.

[4]In classical mythology, the west wind personified.

[5]This piece was another gem written by Chill Hazzard, the long-time and well-known editor. He was a constant "chamber of commerce" advocate for Monongahela and the Valley. Too, he loved to poke fun at Pittsburgh and often sparred editorially with their newspapers.

42

Pittsburgh Daily Post, February 6, 1884
"RAMPANT RIVERS

Another February Flood of Big Dimensions

25 Feet of Water in the Monongahela and Allegheny,
And Both Streams Still Rising Rapidly.

The Signal Service Predicts a Still
Greater Growth of the Flood.

U. S. Signal Corps Office – Pittsburgh, February 6, 1884 -- A special from Washington City at 12:45 this morning, says: 'Heavy rains continue in the Ohio Valley. The river is rising at all points, and is above the danger line at Pittsburgh, Cincinnati and Louisville. Floods will increase, and at the end of the week will reach the mouth of the Ohio river. Give general warning.' – Chas. L. Bozzell, Assistant Observer.

The prediction of the Signal Service published in these columns yesterday morning, that the heavy rains and melting snows would cause a flood in the valleys of the Monongahela, Allegheny and Ohio, was realized yesterday. The general impression among river men is that the flood here will be of as large proportions as that of last February. The Monongahela commenced rising Monday evening, and at 9 o'clock yesterday morning there was 13 feet of water in the channel. At noon, three hours later, there was 20 feet 6 inches. At 11 o'clock last night there was 24 feet, and the stream was rising at the rate of nearly a foot an hour. The maximum depth of water looked for now by river men in this stream is not less than 30 feet, in which event the flood will be the greatest since March 18, 1865, when the Monongahela reached a height of 31 feet 4 inches.

Last night the upper track of the Pittsburgh and Lake Erie railroad, above the Smithfield street bridge, was completely submerged. The P[ittsburgh]., McK[eesport]. & Y[oughiogheny]. was in the same condition, and in addition was so obstructed by driftwood at the intersection of Thirteenth street that trains could not be run. Thirty feet of water will entirely stop all trains on the Lake Erie road. Anyhow, trains were delayed last night by landslides at Point of Rocks and Stoop's Ferry. A number of the iron mills on the South Side was flooded to such an extent that operations have been suspended.

The owners of river craft feel comparatively safe so far. They knew the flood was coming and prepared to meet it. Their vessels are all in good shape, and so secure that they expect no trouble. The only loss reported yesterday was of two loaded coal flats belonging to W. S. Williams. They were in charge of the *Mark Winnett*[1], but broke loose and went over Dam No. 3 [near Elizabeth on the Mon]. The loss is from $1,500 to $2,000. The occupants of business houses along Water street were very active yesterday afternoon removing goods from their cellars preparatory to the inevitable inundation.

The Allegheny river commenced rising at 2 o'clock yesterday morning. At 1 P. M. the marks on the Suspension bridge showed 16½ feet. At 6 o'clock there was 20 feet, at 9 o'clock 23 feet, at midnight 25 feet and rising at the rate of 8 inches an hour. The rapidity with which this river climbed its banks was surprising. At suppertime the dwellers in the low land of the First ward booted at the idea of the water reaching the. When bedtime came they were skirmishing

---

[1]The towboat *Mark Winnett* was built at the Axton yard in W. Brownsville in 1881 for the Marmet Coal Co. When her coal towing days ended, she ended up in Cincinnati where she sank in July, 1899, and was dismantled.

around among their neighbors for a dry spot on which to sleep. On Duquesne way everything that was liable to damage, or to being carried away, was removed to a safer locality. The cellars of the buildings between Duquesne way and Penn avenue were relieved of their contents by those who were awake to the situation, but it is presumed there are many who had no idea of the rapid growth of the flood and its magnitude. The iron mills along the south bank of the Allegheny are always at the mercy of swollen waters, and now as heretofore nothing can be done but make everything secure as possible and calmly watch the encroachments of the resistless tide.

There is trouble all along the north bank of the Allegheny within the limits of Allegheny City, but no special damage is reported. Possession of part of the First ward has been yielded to the river, and many families have vacated their dwellings out of deference to its persistent endeavor to become a temporary occupant. At 7:30 o'clock last evening the corner of Kilbuck and Robinson streets was dry. At nine o'clock it was submerged, and the people living in that locality were navigating the streets in skiffs. South avenue was inundated, and the Exposition ground was several feet under water. Inasmuch as the rain fell nearly all night there is no telling now where the flood will stop.

* * * * * * *

THE HIGH WATER RECORD

Following is the record of big floods in Pittsburgh since 1832:

	Ft.	In.		Ft.	In.
Feb. 10, 1832	35	0	Dec. 14, 1873	25	7
Feb. 10, 1840	26	9	Jan. 8, 1874	22	4
Feb. 1, 1847	26	0	Dec. 30, 1874	21	4
April 19, 1852	31	9	August 3, 1875	21	9
April, 1858	26	0	Dec. 28, 1875	21	8
April 12, 1860	29	7	Sept. 11, 1876	23	7
Jan. 20, 1862	28	7	Dec. 11, 1878	24	6
April 22, 1862	25	4	Jan. 29, 1879	20	0
March 4, 1865	24	0	March 12, 1879	20	0
March 18, 1865	31	4	Feb. 14, 1880	22	0
April 1, 1865	21	6	Feb. 10, 1881	25	0
May 12, 1865	21	6	June 10, 1881	28	0
Feb. 16, 1867	22	0	Jan. 28, 1882	21	9
March 13, 1867	22	6	Feb 22, 1882	21	6
March 18, 1868	22	0	Feb. 5, 1883	25	0
April 15, 1868	20	6	Feb. 8, 1883	27	6
April 11, 1872	20	6			

Capt. Laughlin gives a record of six low water seasons, 1838, 1854, 1856, 1867, 1879, and 1881. In October, 1838, the metal marks at the foot of Wood street showed 9 inches; October 20, 1854, 8 inches; October 20, 1856, 9 inches; September, October and November, 1867, 12 inches. October 21, 1879, new marks at the foot of Market street indicated one inch; September 26, 1881, the bottom of the marks was 1? inches above the water.

* * * * * * *

DESTRUCTION OF THE YOUGH
Towns Inundated and Property Destroyed –
No Lives Lost.

All the tributaries of the Monongahela contributed liberally to the general swell but none became so riotous and unrestrained as the Youghiogheny. This stream is narrow and deep. The current is swift and the valley through which it passes is thickly settled. At a subsequent rise the ice broke and was swept from the headwaters in the mountains to West Newton where a [ice] gorge was formed. This gorge extended from West Newton to Dawson, a distance of twenty miles. The continuous rains of the past two days filled the river bank full. All the creeks and rivulets poured into the main stream, and swelled it to dangerous proportions. The gorge remained immovable. The back water extended as far up the stream as Connellsville, and all the low lands along the route were completely inundated. The little towns and village were swimming around through the country and thousands of dollars worth of property was swept away. No lives were lost, but in almost every town from McKeesport to West Newton, families were compelled to abandon their homes through the second story windows and flee to the hills for safety. West Newton, and especially the western portion of the town, was yesterday morning afloat in about seven feet of water. The paper mills and all the public works were flooded, and all business was entirely suspended. Many of the families residing along the river bank were taken from their houses in skiffs [from?] the second story windows. . . . Several [?] buildings were lifted from their foundations and hurled to splinters in the riotous waters.

About 6 o'clock in the morning the gorge was broken. The waters were still swelling. When the ice moved everything was swept before it. Houses, stables, telegraph poles,

190

and fences all joined in the general break-up and moved slowly towards the Monongahela. Between Elrod's and McKeesport another gorge was formed. This extended back to within about a mile of West Newton. When the ice first moved the water fell about three feet, but the backwater from the second gorge threatened greater danger even than the first. The people who had resumed their homes after the water fell were again compelled to flee for their lives. This almost without warning, and many narrowly escaped being drowned.

At 11 o'clock the gorge again moved. Again destruction and devastation followed in its wake. The current seemed to have grown swifter every hour and when the second break occurred huge mountains of ice were thrown out upon the banks. At many places the ice heaps are higher than the houses. Full grown trees, lumber of every description and various articles of household furniture helped to swell the piles and formed around the monuments of ice a fringe of desolation.

The B[altimore]. & O[hio]. Railroad track was over flowed in several places at points east of West Newton, and travel was considerably delayed. Between West Newton and the mouth of the Big Sewickley all the B. & O. telegraph poles were washed out, and in several places the railroad track is undermined and in a very dangerous condition. The Big Sewickley is also swollen bankful, and its rushing waters add materially to velocity of the Youghiogheny. At the junction of these two streams the country was entirely overflowed and the inhabitants were compelled to leave their houses. The rise was not unexpected to them, and their household goods were removed before they were injured by the water. Many of them stored their goods in the second stories of their dwellings, but many families remained in their house until they were taken from the second story windows in skiffs. One stable was washed away at that point but no other serious damage was reported. At Industry, on the opposite side of the stream, all the houses are flooded but no damage is reported. At Armstrong's the water was up to the second story of the houses. At that point the river is very narrow and the swift current swept everything along the banks, one small frame house, several outbuildings and a stable were carried away. At Buena Vista considerable damage is reported. The inhabitants were taken unawares and their household goods suffered. The flood is said to be the largest at that point for forty years. Along the bank the ice in many places is piled up higher than the houses and many of the houses which are standing several feet in water were held on their foundations by heavy cables coiled around them and fastened to the railroad tracks. Guffey's station was about four feet under water, but the high water was anticipated by the inhabitants, and the destructible property was removed to safe quarters in time to save it. At Robbins' station the people were taken entirely unawares. They knew the river was swelling, but they had no apprehensions of danger. The rise was so sudden and so rapid that the in- habitants barely escaped with their lives. The fall, when it came, was just as sudden and rapid. While one family named Radebaugh were moving their goods in a flatboat from the second story window of their dwelling, the water suddenly dropped and the flatboat, with the family and their household goods, were left high and dry about the center of their garden.

At Coultersville and Suters' station no serious damage is reported, other than both places are flooded with about four feet of water. At both places the provision stores, which are located along the river bank, suffered severely. The residence of Mr. Suter, at Suter's station, was flooded, and his furniture and household goods were damaged.

Bigley's coal tipple at Alpsville was carried away, and at Shaner's station two stables and a small frame house owned by James Maloy were carried down the stream. Dravos' coke tipple at Boston joined the general wreck, which in itself will cause a loss of over $1,000.

Wood, lumber, small buildings, telegraph poles, railroad ties, household furniture and a miscellaneous assortment of articles went crashing and cracking down the stream with the ice, and presented a desolate picture.

* * * * * * *

AT OIL CITY

(Special to the *Pittsburgh Press*)

Oil City, Pa., February 5 – The water rose in the river until 4 P. M., the rise since morning being five feet. Then it fell again, but owing to the breaking of the ice gorges above began rising again. The river has not been within five feet of last year's high water, and the present indications are that it is at its highest. No rain has fallen since noon, and the weather is cool and clear. . . ."

❧

43

Pittsburgh Daily Post, February 7, 1884
(The Flood, Continued)
"34 FEET

The Greatest Swell in the
Triune [three in one] Rivers Since 1832

Pittsburgh and Allegheny
Deluged with Water

People Driven by Thousands
From Their Homes

Acres of Property in Both Cities
Deeply Inundated

Approaches to Most of the
Bridges Submerged

And Communication with
Allegheny City Nearly Severed

Skiff Navigation on Many
Of the Leading Streets

A Call by the Mayor for Help
For the Suffering

The Details of the Greatest
Invasion by Water in
Half a Century

* * * * * * *

HIGH WATER

Feb. 10, 1832	35 feet
April 19, 1852	31 feet, 9 inches
Feb. 6, 1884	33 feet, 9 inches

From the headwaters of the Allegheny in New York and the sources of the Monongahela in the mountains of West Virginia, to Cairo at the mouth of the Ohio, the Ohio valley is today the center of probably the most disastrous and destructive flood that history records. There is every prospect, at this writing, it will exceed in the sweep of its overwhelming and destructive force the historic flood of 1832. The immense snow falls of January, covering the great central States from the summit of the Alleghenies to the Mississippi, has been supplemented by thawing weather and incessant rains, destroying hopes of the gradual melting of the snows, and precipitating this terrible inundation, by letting loose the great reservoirs of our rivers in Western Pennsylvania and West Virginia, with the result that both the Monongahela and Allegheny have become sweeping flood at the same time, throwing such a volume of water into the Ohio that, with the contributions of its other tributaries, the thousand miles of that river will reach its highest recorded stage. This in itself tells the story of losses of property that will run into millions. The vast areas drained by the Ohio and its great feeders from the North and South, are all at the flood stage at the same time. This is something unprecedented, and explains the immensity of the calamity.

The destruction of property and the suffering among the poor along the river banks will be far beyond that of any preceding flood. There is more to destroy. When we had the great inundation of 1832, there were barely 20,000 people in Pittsburgh and Allegheny, and but a small part of the adja-

195

cent river frontage was occupied. Now we have in the two cities a population not far from 300,000 and miles on miles of the river front, far beyond the limits of the two cities, is occupied by great manufacturing enterprises, railways, the dwellings of mechanics and laborers, and varied branches of business and industry, representing immense investments and employment of labor. All this has been inundated, and the waters have forced their way to the principal business streets, far outside the danger line. There has been some brief time for preparation for the inevitable, by telegraphic reports of the approaching floods, yet the reality so far outstripped preparation that the losses and suffering promise to be appalling. In 1832 the flood announced itself – brought its own card, so to speak. There were no weather reports – no telegraphic or other warnings – and people who went to bed on the night of the 9th of February, unconscious of danger, were awakened by the rushing of mighty waters and the flooding of their homes. They had no warning. Science has improved on that.

To group the main facts of the local situation, the river at this writing is reported at 34 feet and rising at the rate of two or three inches an hour. This is the Monongahela mark, with which comparisons are made. The highest point recorded, February 10, 1832, is 35 feet, and in the next greatest flood, in 1852, the pier mark showed 31 feet 9 inches. Between Penn street and the Allegheny the streets are all inundated, cellars flooded, the first stories of dwellings and stores have one and two feet of water in them. Penn street is navigable in skiffs from the railroad crossing at Thirteenth street to Water. Horne's store, in the Library Hall building, has two feet of water in its large salesroom. On Water street, at Wood, the water is nearly up to First street, and from Ferry, the Point is inundated in varying depths. The cellars on Fifth avenue, Wood, Market and Liberty streets are flooded. Communication with the bridges to Allegheny is by wagon or boat. All that part of Allegheny City south of the Fort Wayne railroad track back from the approaches of the bridge to Seminary Hill is under water. This includes a large part of the business section of the city; but, in addition, the river front of the Allegheny is submerged from Herr's Island to Woods' Run. In the two cities it is certain that there are thousands of people who have been flooded out of their homes.

The great manufacturing establishments that line the three rivers for miles have suspended operations, and thousands of artisans and laborers are idle. In some cases, although not many, valuable plants have been much injured. All the railroads along the rivers have been compelled to suspend operations, or have been much embarrassed and delayed. Industrial establishments in the heart of the city have suspended, owing to the overflow of cellars from the sewers.

Great crowds thronged the streets bordering the booming rivers; and it was pleasant to note the general exhibition of good humor and desire to help those needing help. Novel enterprises sprung into existence out of the necessities of the hour, in the transportation of persons and property. All other business was at a standstill.

* * * * * * *

1884 FLOOD: Liberty Hall,
corner of Sixth St. & Pennsylvania Avenue.
Source: *Harper's Weekly, February 23, 1884, p. 124.*
Pennsylvania Room, Carnegie Library.

RELIEF FOR THE NEEDY AND HOMELESS

No estimate can be made of the number of unfortunates who will be thrown on the generosity of the people by this terrible visitation. It will run into the thousands, and all cases demand prompt attention. Mayor Lyon yesterday, with admirable and energetic good sense, made the best provision possible in the City Hall and other public places for the homeless and needy. He will be sustained in this by the characteristic generosity of our citizens. Those who have not suffered in person or property should esteem it a privilege as well as a duty to contribute to their unfortunate and needy neighbors. Pittsburgh has done good work in subscribing to aid sufferers at the South and elsewhere from calamities of a similar character, and we have no question will excel its record in doing what needs to be done, and doing it promptly in aid of our own people who have lost their all, and are in want of the shelter and common necessaries of life. A public meeting has been called for half-past three o'clock this afternoon to make an effective organization to push on the good work.

* * * * * * *

BETWEEN THE RIVERS
What A *Post* Reporter Saw Along the Wharves

At seven o'clock in the morning the gauge on the Monongahela wharf marked 29 feet 2 inches. The wharf boats and steamers hugged Water street and the merchants and business men along that thoroughfare began looking to the safety of the goods stored in their cellars. The water was just touching the street, but the indications were of an alarming nature. Everybody was excited. Many were alarmed, and the stalwart river men shuddered at the monstrous proportions of the stream. Men hurried hither and thither along the street. Women and children huddled together and stood shivering on the street corners. Some shouted gleefully at the rushing water gradually swept towards them and covered the street. Others with a keener sense of the destruction and disaster being wrought, wept from fright. In an hour later the gauge was covered with water, and every cellar from the B. & O. depot to the Suspension bridge at Sixth street was flooded. The Stockdale wharf-boat had moved up to the telegraph poles at Wood and Water street. The street car tracks at that point were under water, and every cellar up Wood street to Fourth avenue was more or less under water. Notwithstanding the warning given, many of the Wood street merchants were taken unawares, and suffered materially in consequence. Others were more active, and when the water reached them they were prepared for it. Their goods had been removed to the first floor of their business places where they were supposed to be out of harm's way. In this they were mistaken and before another hour many were compelled to move their wares to their second floor to save them. The water had not yet touched Wood street, but the backwater in the sewers was doing all the damage. When the sewers began to overflow the low cellars and basements filled up so rapidly that it was almost impossible to save anything that had been left unremoved.

The inundation from the Monongahela was not confined to Water street but extended up the stream to the City Farm. All that expanse of low land was flooded by several feet of water. The inhabitants of that section were compelled to abandon their homes during the early hours of yesterday morning. A goodly portion of their household goods was taken with them, but what was left was either swept away or destroyed by the water. Many of the little tenement houses are entirely under water, and others are in the water to their roofs. The Soho coke ovens are completely lost to sight, and flatboats and barges are floating over them. The water extends up to Second avenue, and the desolate picture was made, if possible, more dreary looking by the flickering gas in the lamps at either side of the street. They were lighted on Tuesday evening, but yesterday morning it was impossible to get to them, and they burned and flickered all day. The hills and highlands overlooking Second avenue were thronged all day with thousands of people. Many of them were residents of the little houses in the valley. They watched the water rising, and many of them saw their household furniture floating away. Women wept over the distressing picture. Children cried for joy as they saw their houses disappearing under the water, and strong men, many of them puddlers and mill workers, stood by and in silence suffered and sighed.

At 1:30 in the afternoon there was 30 feet 3 inches in the Monongahela channel. The floating property along the wharf had moved up, and was afloat about the middle of Water street. The water had crossed the street entirely, and was gradually making its way up Wood street. The first floor of Fairman & Henderson's boat store was now flooded with about an inch of water. Their goods were all saved, however, as most of their stuff was removed to the second story while some of their hay and grain was ferried across the street and was stored in the Stockdale wharfboat. The river now extended from the buildings fronting to Water street to beyond the Lake Erie railroad on the opposite side. The electric lights along the wharf have always been a benefit, but during Tuesday night their presence was of incalculable value to the river men.

* * * * * * *

THE ALLEGHENY

The scene on the Pittsburgh side of the Allegheny wharf, from the mouth of the Ohio to the Sharpsburg bridge, was more desolate than along the Monongahela. The damage, too, is much greater. The wharf is used as a storing place for lumber and property of all kinds. All this was supposed to be safely harbored, but the enormous stage of water rendered all precautionary measures useless. The current in this stream was unusually swift, and the channel was running full of ice. The rise was sudden and rapid. Everything within reach was carried away. Huge piles of lumber, rafts of logs and barges of coal were jammed together in the general rush and were ground to splinters. Houses were flooded along the route. Valuable household property was washed away or destroyed, and devastation is spread all along the stream.

This stream was rising rapidly at the headwaters all day. The Clarion and Redbank, and several other of its tributaries, put out their ice and were continuing liberally to the general swell. Damage is reported all along the stream from Parkers to this city, and to watch the drift in the stream as it went crushing, grinding and roaring under the Suspension bridge told the sad story of a general sweep. Small stacks of hay, shocks of corn, cord wood and even farming utensils mingled with the huge cakes of ice and hurried to join the wrecks and ruins from the Monongahela and its tributaries. It was reported once during the afternoon that the Kittanning bridge had been carried away. This rumor created considerable apprehension for the safety of the bridge spanning the river at this point. The Mechanics street bridge was said to be in an alarming condition even before noon and as the stage of water increased, its condition became more dangerous. It was thought if the Mechanics street bridge was swept away the Hand street structure would be carried with it and in this event the Suspension bridge at Sixth street was not considered strong enough to withstand the crash. The bridge at the Point was eagerly watched during the day. Had any of the others been moved its destruction would necessarily have followed. Towards evening, when the waters seemed to have reached the limit, and the bridges were all left standing, there was a feeling of relief spread among those who had watched the structures all day.

At the Point, where the riotous waters of the Allegheny and Monongahela met, there was a general struggle for admission to the Ohio. Both fought desperately, and in the conflict the water s were forced up all the streets leading in that direction. In consequence, all the property along the Point, and between Liberty street and Duquesne way was completely submerged. All the houses in that portion of the city have basement kitchens. All these were flooded, and in many places the water invaded the second floor. No preparations had been made for this stage of water, and when it came many families were forced to the upper stories of their dwellings leaving their furniture of the second floors floating about in water ranging in depth from ten inches to 3 feet. At the Point the greatest excitement prevailed. Many of the inhabitants were too frightened to remain in their houses. The water was too high for them to get out from their first floors and not high enough to allow them to escape from the second stories. In this way they were penned in with death and destruction staring them in the face. Men were floating about in skiffs and flatboats, assuring the inhabitants of their perfect safety as long as they remained in the second story of their dwellings, but even this failed to allay their fears. There seemed to be no attention paid to the vast amount of property being destroyed. Everybody was anxious about their lives and the lives of their friends and everything else was allowed to drift about at will.

During the afternoon a freight train was pushed down Liberty street to Thirty-eighth street. This was used by thousands of people as a means to get near their homes. From the end of the train they were taken in boats and wagons to their homes. In the turmoil and excitement yesterday it was impossible to even estimate the damage. Everybody within reach of the water suffered. The hay market was entirely out of sight, and several wagons with small loads of hay were carried off. The Robinson House, at Duquesne way and Seventh street, is flooded with about two feet of water. The entire ground floor was last night occupied by a portion of the Allegheny. The doors were forced open, the first floor windows were broken and the hostelry was transformed into a harbor for drift and debris of every description. Others places along Duquesne way were equally unfortunate and until the water falls it will be utterly impossible to even attempt to fix the loss.

At about three o'clock in the afternoon the gauge on the Allegheny river was lost to sight. The stream was still swelling but the rise was much slower than during the early part of the day. The decrease in the rapidity of the rise is due to the broad surface which has to be covered, and not to any decrease in the volume of water that is being forced into the river by the streams above. Rivermen find great difficulty in getting reports from the upriver towns. The telegraph companies report their lines down in all directions. The railroads are experiencing the same difficulty. The lines are being put in shape as fast as possible, however.

The Pittsburgh gas works out Second avenue were completely submerged early yesterday afternoon, and the gas was turned off before dark. The works at Pipetown were untouched, but the Consolidated works out Penn avenue were furnishing plenty of gas at a late hour last night. But much of the city was in darkness. Many of the business places that keep open all night were lighted with flickering candles, that seemed to be frightened nervous by an occasional glimpse of an electric light. The Allegheny Light Company kept their lights burning all night, and with a combination of electricity and the old-time tallow candle the city did fairly well for light.

At 10 o'clock last night the stage of water in the Monongahela was 33 feet 2 inches and still swelling slowly. The difficulty in securing information from the headwaters made it difficult for the rivermen to even predict the full extent of the rise here. The boatmen, however, generally agreed that the swell would continue until this evening, at which time they thought the record would be beaten, to do which would require over 35 feet of water.

At 10 o'clock the Monongahela had reached some distance up Wood street, and the Transverse street cars only went as far as Fourth avenue.

Following is the record of the hourly rise in the Monongahela yesterday, as kept by Fairman & Henderson:

Time	Feet	Inches
7:30 A.M.	29	2
8:30 A.M.	29	9
9:30 A.M.	30	3
10:00 A.M.	30	3
11:00 A.M.	31	-
11:30 A.M.	31	2½
12:00 M.	31	4½
12:30 P.M.	31	1
1:05 P.M.	31	9½
1:30 P.M.	31	11
2:30 P.M.	32	2
3:00 P.M.	32	2
3:30 P.M.	32	5
4:30 P.M.	35	9
10:00 P.M.	33	2

The backing up of water through the sewer connections of the lower portions of the city is responsible for a very considerable amount of damage. At 1 o'clock in the afternoon the Penn avenue sewers began to overflow and in less than twenty minutes Sixth street, from Liberty street, to the Suspension bridge was submerged. An immense crowd of people gathered at the junction of Liberty and Sixth streets to watch the peculiar antics of those having occasion to cross Penn avenue. Soon the water was too deep to be waded, even by those who wore gum boots, and then the energetic hackmen put in an appearance. Ferries in the shape of express wagons crowded the street from one end to the other, and as the water increased the number or conveyances in which to cross it increased with it. The spectators increased too and in an hour after the water appeared on the street, the jam was so great that even the horses and wagons were unable to get through. A number of people with gum boots were bold enough to wade out in the stream to their waists. A misstep would plunge them head first into the water. This furnished unlimited amusement for the lookers on, and one shout followed another until the greatest confusion prevailed and the police found it necessary to force the crowd back. To do this it was necessary to secure a rope. By stretching it across the street and attaching a policeman to either end the street was entirely cleared. Travel by horse cars between Pittsburgh and Allegheny was suspended before 2 o'clock. For a time the passengers were transferred by boats from one car to another, but that was soon abandoned, and all those who desired to get to or from Allegheny, were left to the tender care of the enterprising expressmen. 'Here you are now! A trip across the ocean for a nickel! Here you are now! Your last chance!' This was the song sung by them. Many people invested the nickel in the ride more to feel the sensation of crossing the ocean as it was called than from necessity. Before three o'clock Penn avenue from Thirteenth street to the river was submerged. Library Hall was flooded and Horne's store was knee deep in water. All the other business places, along that thoroughfare between the points mentioned were equal sufferers. The Penn Avenue Street Car Company did not suspend business until the water was high enough to enter the cars. The first floor of the Museum was last night standing in three feet of water, but the place was still open. The audience was limited to the employees.

About three o'clock in the afternoon, when the crowd about Sixth and Liberty street was the biggest, a fire broke out in Scott & Co.'s fancy goods store, on Sixth street. A still alarm was sent in, but when the department responded the most intense excitement prevailed among the crowd. Nobody knew where the fire was, and everybody rushed wildly about trying to find it. Before even the engines found it the fire was gotten under control, but the excitement was not allayed until long after.

The St. Clair Hotel suffered only in its restaurant department. Although the water was within a few inches of the door it did not enter. The boarders who an hour before had walked into their dinner were taken back to their places of business in skiffs.

The engine room of the *Times* office on Liberty street was inundated. On Penn street, Sixth street, Liberty street from the river to the Union Depot, Market street, Wood street from Water to Diamond alley, the cellars were all filled, but most of the valuable goods were removed in time to prevent heavy loss. At the Duquesne Depot hundreds of teams were engaged in removing goods, which had been stored there, while men on boats recovered valuable property from a train of freight cars which had been left on a siding on Water street.

Thus far the flood has been unattended with loss of life. Several drownings were reported, but on investigation proved all such reports to be unfounded. An unusual number of narrow escapes were made however, especially in the vicinity of the Point. One mishap occurred to a wagon crossing the overflow at Sixth street. About eighteen passengers were on the wagon, ten of whom were females. In some way the wagon was upset, throwing the whole load into the water, which was then about 2 feet deep. At ten o'clock last night the water had risen almost to the wagon boxes. Large cakes of ice were floating about, which rendered it almost impossible for a horse to get through.

* * * * * * *

ON THE SOUTH SIDE
Twelve Feet of Water on Bingham Street, and Havoc Generally Everywhere

The overflowing Monongahela is working sad havoc among the mills and residences that line its banks on the South Side. Work is suspended in nearly all the factories. Most of them being completely flooded and those situated above the present water line are being fast put into condition to better receive the on-coming torrent. Bingham street is entirely submerged so far west as Ninth street, the water in many places being more than twelve feet above the pavement.

Most of the families being obliged to flee from their homes and leave everything behind them. It was not an uncommon sight yesterday to see boats being paddled along at an even height with the second story of many of the flooded houses, rescuing the inmates, who had no thought of taking any of their household goods with them, thankful for the opportunity to escape with their lives.

The few boats and rafts plying along the streets were in constant demand, and although heroic efforts were made to comply with every request for aid, the inhabitants clung to their houses to such a late hour that when they began to leave, the calls for boats grew so numerous they could not receive proper attention. Several persons, frantic with fear, after calling loudly for assistance and receiving none, jumped from their windows and swam to dry ground. Business of all kinds along the river is entirely suspended, and the fear that the worst is yet to come has grown to such an extent that merchants and tradesmen generally are conveying their goods from places of comparative safety to shelter at an elevation beyond possible destruction from water.

The tracks of the Lake Erie railroad are overflowed as far west as Middletown, both freight and passenger trains being entirely stopped, no trains having been run since midnight Tuesday. The depth of the water on the track just below the depot at twelve o'clock last night was more than thirteen feet.

The condition of the P[ittsburgh], McK[eesport] & Y[oughiogheny] railroad is little better than that of the Lake Erie, no trains being run between here and McKeesport, the water above the Tenth street bridge being high enough above the tracks to almost entirely conceal from view an engine which was disabled last night while being taken on its way to a place of safety.

A curious spectacle is to be seen at the lumber yard of Murphy & Diebold, above the Smithfield street bridge. Precautionary measures were taken on Monday; the piles of lumber were tightly bound with ropes and fastened to stakes driven in the ground. Heretofore the measure had proved a successful protection against high water, but as the flood increased yesterday, and the bulk of water grew to a sufficient depth to float the heavy piles of lumber, they broke their fastenings as though they had been made of thread, and falling in with the rush of the current, were carried swiftly down the river. Some of the smaller piles remained in the yard, and in company with a number of sheds and out-buildings, continue to float through the yard. The damage will reach fully $5,000. At the upper end of this yard is the office and storeroom of the Phoenix Facing Company. The first floor of which contains the crude stock of the firm, the engine and all the machinery, and as the water is almost on a level with the flooring of the second story, the stock will be a complete loss and the machinery considerably damaged.

Fred Fichtel's storeroom and George Nevergold's carriage works at this point are both filled with water.

The glass works of A. & D. H. Chambers, between Fifth and Sixth streets, are damaged to the extent of more than $10,000.

The South Pittsburgh Planing Mill is flooded to the depth of several feet. Loss about $2,000.

The machine shop of Robinson, Rea & Co., is badly damaged.

The Republican Iron Works shut down at 12 o'clock on account of the pumps being covered with water. No damage is anticipated.

There is six feet of water in the iron works of Oliver Bros. & Phillips, and a great loss is looked for.

The residence of J. M. Scott, foot of Twelfth street is completely submerged.

The engines in the Water Works are under water, and the supply of water has been shut off.

Jos. Finch & Co.'s distillery is deluged to the depth of nine or ten feet.

Abel, Smith & Co.'s glass works is flooded. Two hundred tons of soda and salt coke ruined by the water.

Among the heaviest losers are the McKee Bros., their glass works at Eighteenth street being completely flooded. Twenty-seven pots filled with glass are under water. About 2 o'clock yesterday afternoon a fire broke out in a lime shed connected with their works, but was extinguished before any damage was done.

Young's saw mill on Thirtieth street is filled with water. The damage will be great.

Jones & Laughlins' pattern shop, Thirtieth street, presents a drowned-out appearance. Work has been suspended in their other shops, but they have not been flooded.

Several families living on boats at the foot of Thirtieth street barely escaped drowning and were obliged to leave all their effects behind them.

Three cars loaded with lime were standing on the track at Oliver & Roberts' wire mill. When the water reached the bottom of the cars they took fire, and fears were entertained that the flames would set fire to the warehouse of Dilworth, Porter & Co. A fire alarm was sent out, but when the firemen arrived upon the scene they found the cars could not be reached without the aid of a boat. While they were in search of one some of the wire-workers succeeded in knocking in the roof of the cars from the top of the wire shops and extinguished the fire.

A frame house situated at the foot of Eighth street was carried away from its foundation and went floating down the rivers.

Two boys engaged in catching drift wood had their boat upset and were on the point of drowning when they were rescued by some men who witnessed the accident and started out in a boat after them. A woman by the name of Donnelly [?], while in the act of passing over a temporary bridge constructed over an excavation on Seventeenth street, fell into the water and was rescued with considerable difficulty.

There is fully four feet of water in the P. McK. & Y. railroad tunnel. Especial care was taken to build the tunnel above the scope of high water.

Great quantities of lumber have been carried away from the yard of Phillips & Mittenzwer. The cooper shop and lumber yard are entirely submerged.

Work has stopped at Chase [?], Cook & Co.'s mill, the place being filled with water.

All the ice in the houses belonging to Fred. Vallowe [?] and the Monongahela Ice Company is completely destroyed.

A.M. Byers & Co.'s pipe mill is filled with water.

The water is encroaching Carson street all the way from the Smithfield bridge to Limerick. The mills between these points are all flooded and the inhabitants of houses were obliged to move out early.

* * * * * * *

ALLEGHENY INUNDATED
A Deplorable State of Affairs on
the North Side

At least one half of the low lands of Allegheny were inundated. The rise was so unexpected that few people managed to remove any property to a place of safety and a large number were compelled to live in the second story of their houses, and travel to and from land in skiffs. At 10:45 in the morning the marks showed 30 feet 6 inches, and the water rose steadily, contrary to expectations. The river bank was changed to the West Penn railroad track, and it was lined with people. The river front presented a curious spectacle. The Exposition grounds were the bottom of the river, and the water swept over it rapidly, not having the huge building to retard its progress, as in other floods. River avenue could not be distinguished from the river, and barges and boats of all kinds were manned to the second story windows of houses. The people on the avenue and adjoining streets were compelled to move out during the night, leaving their household goods at the mercy of the water. Many had difficulty in finding places to stay. Those who took refuge in the second stories of their houses could not secure food, and were compelled to abandon their dwellings.

The scene on the streets when the water began to overflow there was one of the utmost confusion. Men, women and children were doing all in their power to remove as much of the household goods as possible before being damaged by the muddy water. All kinds of vehicles and improvised boats were used to carry goods to places of safety. A number of men made rafts from the timbers of sheds and sold them to the unfortunate families at $2 each. They were used to good advantage. On School street, near River avenue, the water poured into the second stories of houses. Many rafts collided while being poled along the streets. Several were broken and their cargoes of furniture spilled out into the water. Some people whose houses are situated on knolls lived apparently very comfortably in the second story. A horse was found tied in a stable on Lacock street with the water up to its neck. It was removed with difficulty.

The residents of Herr's Island wisely moved out of their dwellings during the night; they were compelled to leave their furniture. The police assisted the people on Killbuck street to vacate in skiffs. Those in indigent circumstances were taken to the Mayor's office and provided for by the Mayor. At noon the water was 13 feet deep in the Coliseum building. The floor, stage and a piano were floating about. The waters poured into the windows of Calonnade Row and other buildings on Federal street at ten o'clock, and the places were accessible only by boats. Wagons could be drawn through with difficulty, the horses being compelled to swim. The wagon beds floated when empty, and when laden could not be drawn. The street cars were stopped only after the water flooded the interior of the cars. Great difficulty was then experienced in reaching Pittsburgh.

The first expressman who started to haul passengers across the bridge charged twenty-five cents for the trip. In a short time a number of other express wagons were engaged carrying passengers at five cents each. Many amusing incidents occurred. Several wagons broke down and scattered their occupants into the water. Shortly after noon the gas company announced that the works were inundated and no gas could be made. What was left in the tanks would not last long, and consumers should secure candles and oil. A wild rush for candles then ensued, and in a short time there was a scarcity of the article. Coal was also very scarce, and none could be secured from the yards.

Large crowds stood on the banks watching the flood. The river was full of ice, logs, boards, portions of rafts and houses. Much of the debris was washed to the shore. The Sixteenth street bridge was reported unsafe in the morning, and no person was allowed to cross it, as the water almost touched the floor. Large quantities of debris lodged against the piers of the structure, but they managed to bear the pressure. The Ewalt street bridge was also expected to succumb, and it was feared that if it gave way it would carry the other bridges along. The Ft. Wayne Railroad bridge was crowded with heavy engines and cars in order to keep it in position and save it in case any of the upper bridges were swept against it.

Hundreds of men and boys stood on the bridge peering up the stream and rushing to the different piers when they would observe an unusually large cake of ice, a log or a lot of driftwood rapidly coming down. The current was so swift that when anything struck the pier there was a report loud enough to be heard on either side of the river, and the object striking the pier would immediately sink, to rise probably thirty or forty feet below the bridge.

A large mass of lumber passed under the Suspension bridge from Herr's Island about one o'clock, causing a stampede on the structure. The water was over 6 feet deep at the north end of the Union bridge, and that part of the Allegheny was simply a bay reaching from Birmingham to Seminary Hill – a mass of turbulent waters. The southern section of the city suffered the most.

The water made its way through Isabella, Robinson and Lacock streets, and was only stopped by the embankment of the West Penn road. Federal street, being higher than the others, kept the flood back to the alley between Robinson and Lacock, but on Morgan and all adjoining thoroughfares it rushed clear up to the track, burying fully one-half the city beneath it. The southern section of town suffers the most, so far as extent of ground covered goes, but the whole first plateau of the city is under water. The wards that are the most drowned out are the First, Fourth, Fifth, Sixth, and Eighth.

Probably every family residing between River avenue and the Ft. Wayne railroad sustained more or less damage. All were rendered homeless. On South avenue the houses were in about fifteen feet of water. The Union and Rebecca street car lines were compelled to stop running early in the day. The people appeared to be prepared for the rise in Woods Run and Manchester, and not much damage was done. Oliver's lower mill and the ark house mill were submerged. Two shanty boats [?] by the boys employed at the Superior Rail Mill as loading shanties were carried away. Along the Ft. Wayne Railroad at the different stations, especially at Ellsworth, the houses in the hollows are under water. At Freedom the track was covered and damaged. The cellar of the Government building at Bellevue was filled and the people living in the houses along the shore compelled to move.

Trains on the West Penn Railroad were delayed by an extensive landslide at Livermore. The track was covered with water at Tarentum, and trains were only run to Springdale. The cellar of the Federal street depot was filled with water.

The Pittsburgh and Western railroad was entirely submerged along the line, and no trains were run. The depot was also flooded.

The most prominent factories flooded were the Westinghouse Air Brake Company, Penn Cotton Mill, Eagle Cotton Mill, Banner Lead Works, the Scrap Iron Works, Reynold's & Co.'s Bolt and Nut Works, Bradley's Woolen Mills, Siebert & Co.'s furniture factory, and several other industries that employ quite a number of hands. The number of males and females thrown at least temporarily out of employment will exceed eight thousand. The number of idle working people on the street indicted the extent to which labor suffered. In the cotton and woolen mills the waters reach nearly half way up the first story, and much damage will be done machinery and goods stored on these floors and in their basements.

The wife of a German employed at Klages' glue factory, who resided in a house near the corner of Grantham and Lacock streets, gave premature birth to a child during the excitement. The child was to have been buried during the afternoon, but the flood interfered with the funeral. The neighbors took charge of the mother.

As far as could be learned no casualties occurred. James G. Weyman upset in a skiff and had a narrow escape from drowning. A little boy and girl named Percy Rinehart and Ida Farran strayed away from home and it is thought they may have been drowned.

216

The inundated district of Allegheny varies in width from one to five squares, and is the most thickly populated section of the city. Within its limits live the majority of the working people, whose dwellings are packed close together; and each one, from the apartments in the big tenements to the little frame, is the home of one, two and sometimes three families.

Mayor Peterson distributed his whole day force and part of the night force through the flooded districts, directing them when informed of a flooded home where the inmates were anxious to leave to take possession of the first boat they saw and rescue the endangered ones and their goods. Invaluable service was rendered in this way, and the police saved many families and large quantities of goods. In several instances families were found who, though in close quarters, refused absolutely to leave their houses.

The Hope and Ellsworth engine houses were under water at an early hour. The former company was moved to the stables of the Allegheny Express Company, on Sandusky street, and the latter to the Grant engine house. The water was of height sufficient to endanger the fire alarm boxes. A detail of firemen was sent out in skiffs to take down all boxes along the river front and in the lower part of the city – thirty-six in number.

The letter carriers, whose routes are in the submerged district, delivered yesterday's mails in skiffs. A large number of letter boxes were found to be completely filled with water, while others held just enough to destroy the mail that had been deposited the day before. Toward evening the sole route open for communication between the cities was the P[ittsburgh]., Ft. W[ayne]. & C[hicago]. railroad bridge. The pressure of foot passengers became so great that the railroad company stopped running freight trains to allow as much of their bridge as possible to the people. A drunken colored man staggered upon the bridge about three o'clock. He chose to walk up on the cross ties. When in the middle he lost his balance and fell between the ties. His arm caught on the rail, and there he hung, his feet dampened by the surging waters, stupidly staring around until several men bodily lifted him to his feet.

The Chestnut street bridge was closed to passengers early in the day. The ice hammered and ground under the floor of the bridge till it trembled from end to end. It appeared, with the exception of one of two holes in the floor, to be in good condition, but as it is believed that the heavy timber arches have been displaced or broken, the gates were closed to everyone. The Ninth street bridge was also in a condition far from satisfactory, and it, too, was closed.

* * * * * * *

CONDITION OF RAILROADS
They Are All Disabled Except the
Pennsylvania Central

Yesterday afternoon a representative of *The Post* visited the various depots to ascertain the condition of the different railroads leading out of the city, and find out as to the regularity with which trains were being moved, and the probable damage done. At the Lake Erie office it was learned that no trains had been started out on that road since nine o'clock yesterday morning, the tracks being entirely inundated all along the line, and from the present outlook of affairs no trains will be able to leave within the next twenty-four hours, unless there is a sudden fall. Quite a number of washouts and slides are reported all along the road, but no serious damage has been reported. General Passenger Agent Smith, whom the reporter called upon yesterday afternoon at his office on the South Side, appeared to take in the situation with apparent unconcern, and looked as though the flood was but a matter of course, and that all would be right in the course of time. He said the damage so far reported was very light, but there is no telling what the condition of the track would be when the water subsides. He thought that when the water drops to twenty-seven feet travel can be immediately resumed unless some accident has occurred which is not known of now. News from along the line is very meager and hard to get, owing to the telegraph wires being down. However, station agents who have been heard from report everything submerged, but no serious damage as yet. There is no doubt but what considerable track will have to be repaired before travel can be resumed with safety.

Travel on the Pittsburgh, McKeesport and Youghiogheny, which is operated by the Lake Erie Company, is entirely at a stand still, and no trains have been started out on the road since early yesterday morning. The track is entirely overflowed about the South side, and a number of slides and washouts are reported all along the line, but no serious mishaps have been reported.

When the reporter called at the Baltimore and Ohio depot, at Grant and Water streets, he experienced considerable difficulty in finding out anything in regard to the condition of that road. One official reported the road all right and trains running regularly, while another reported slides and washouts all along the line. However, by persistent struggling around for an hour or more, it was learned that no through trains had been started out since early yesterday morning, and but few accommodations were trying to run, as the road in some places is entirely submerged, and tracks have been damaged to some extent in several places. A large force of workmen have been out along the road all day fixing up the tracks where washouts had occurred, but as soon as one place could be repaired trouble would break out somewhere else. Supt. King started out over the road early yesterday morning, but up to a late hour last night had not been heard from. The telegraph wires are down in a good many places, and it is almost impossible to ascertain any facts concerning the exact condition of the road much further than McKeesport. Train No. 2 from Baltimore, due in this city at 7:14 yesterday morning, reported at McKeesport at 11:30 A. M., and up to a late hour last night had not yet arrived here. When the reporter visited the B. & O. ticket office, at Fifth avenue and Wood street, Ticket Agent Gregory informed him that he was selling tickets to everybody who inquired for them, with the understanding that the passengers would have to run all risks as to trains leaving the city on time. Quite a number of tickets for local trains were sold, but very few through tickets were disposed of.

A collision occurred at Port Perry yesterday morning between the West Newton train west and a train east. The engines were badly damaged and the passengers badly shaken up, but no person was seriously injured.

The principal part of the water is reported out of the Youghiogheny at McKeesport, and the large amount of water in the Monongahela is caused by back water from the Allegheny.

In answer to an interrogation as to the condition of the Pennsylvania Central railroad Train Master Butler said:

'My young friend, what do you suppose the condition of a road which is built upon a solid rock bed is in? Why, the Pennsylvania Central is in excellent condition, and all trains are running regular. It will take something worse than this to stop travel on this road.'

On the Panhandle trains have been running all day, with but few delays. Trains on the Fort Wayne are running regular to Baden, Beaver county, but at Freedom there is a general blockade, and it is impossible to pass that point. On the Pittsburgh and Cleveland, and Erie and Pittsburgh, trains were running yesterday but were taken off last night, and will not resume again until the water recedes. All through trains have been taken off the Fort Wayne road, and no trains left on that road last night.

The regular Chicago limited mail over the Fort Wayne and Chicago left for Chicago last night at nine o'clock over the Panhandle route.

The Pittsburgh, Virginia and Charleston road is experiencing no difficulty in running trains, except that they are delayed somewhat by small washouts and slides.

Trains on the West Penn road are running regularly to Freeport, but are stopped there on account of the bridge which spans the Allegheny at this point being in a dangerous condition.

* * * * * * *

THE FLOODED MILLS
The Extent To Which Manufacturing
Establishments Have Suffered

The mills, workshops and factories of all kinds situated on the banks of both rivers on the flood line are submerged. On the Allegheny Carnegie Bros. Union mills, the Black Diamond steel works, Shoenberger's mills, nail factories and furnace, Zug's mill, the Crescent steel works, Hussey, Binns & Co., the Crucible works, Hussey, Howe & Co., the Pittsburgh Steel Casting Company, the Star Fire Brick works, Armstrong's Cork factory, in fact every mill and workshop that lines that river had to close down yesterday morning and thousands of men were thrown idle. Some were kept about the mills to save property. The most serious damage will in all probability be suffered by Shoenberger & Co. The warehouse of this firm, in which was stored many tons of finished iron and nails, packed ready for shipment, is deluged. The blast furnace of Shoenberger, Speer & Co., above Fifteenth street, which has been banked for the past week on account of a strike, is in danger of being blow up by the water reaching the heated portions of the furnace. All the mills and factories along he Monongahela out Second avenue were entirely submerged. Business was suspended on Tuesday evening. The water was then high enough to drown out the lines. Yesterday morning the mills were several feet deep in water, but last night they stood in water to the roofs. Huge cakes of ice, lumber and drift floated into the second story windows. The Keystone Rolling mill has four feet of water on the floor of the works, while the Copper Works, Crescent Steel Works, Soho Iron Works and other establishments are literally drowned out. The coke works of Robison & Co., were enveloped yesterday morning in a bank of steam, the water having reached the fires in the ovens and destroyed the charges in process of coking. At the Soho planing mills, above the ovens, considerable loss was sustained by the floating off of lumber, and the destruction of finished stock which was stored on the ground floor of the mill. Moorhead & Co. were trying to raise some of their most valuable machinery above the water by means of pulleys. When one of the managers was asked what their loss would be, he said he could form no idea.

At the Oliver Wire Mill on the South Side considerable damage was done by the water covering the machinery and annealing pits. On Birmingham street and Chestnut alley about twenty-five houses are filled almost to the second story. Considerable lumber was carried away from the South Side Planing Mill yards. About 11 o'clock three cars of lime belonging to the Oliver & Roberts Wire Company caught fire, and as it was feared that the flames would communicate to the mill, a still alarm was sent into the Mechanics Hose Company, which responded but could not get a line of hose to the cars as they were in eight feet of water. The fire was extinguished by a small hose manned by several men in a skiff. The cars and their contents were entirely destroyed.

Finch's distillery and warehouse is under water and the damage cannot be estimated. The houses on Chestnut street from Third to First avenue are filled with water to the first floor. A number of people are living in the second story of their houses and using a skiff to get to and from land. The horses in the Transfer Company's stables were remanded to a place of safety early this morning. The fire in the furnace at Watterson & Co.'s stained glass works on First street was extinguished at noon. Although there is ten feet of water in Atterbury & Co.'s glass factory work is still progressing. The damage to the stock will not be heavy. At Able, Smith & Co.'s window glass factory the water is two feet deep in the furnaces. Kim's Row was also inundated. About $3,000 worth of lumber was swept away from Murphy & Diebold's lumber yard above the Smithfield street bridge. The water is about fifteen feet below the flooring of the bridge, showing that the old structure would have undoubtedly been swept away.

The water extinguished the fires in two of the Siemens furnaces of McKee Bros., causing a direct loss of from $4,000 to $6,000, and a consequential damage of three week's delay. This is true of many other mills. The fact is the magnitude of the flood is so great that comparatively little in the way of satisfactory details as to the extent of damage to manufactories can be accrued.

* * * * * * *

THE DRAMATIC FEATURES
The Comedy Element of the Watery
Invasion – Scenes and Incidents

To relate all that came under the reportorial eye in the way of scenes and incidents would require more time and room than is now at command. Martin O'Toole, brother of Officer O'Toole, was an active worker and rendered valuable assistance to those in the First ward who were unable to do the necessary work alone. In his zeal to get a feather-bed out of one of the rooms he rolled a baby up in it and was a hundred yards away from the house before his attention was attracted by the smothered cries. From another house he took a bundle of bed clothing and a sauce pan. When he had placed them where they would be safe the owner soundly berated him because he had allowed the bottom of the pan to come in contact with something. An Irishman dropped a frying pan and dove after it for full ten minutes before he recovered the treasure, and was tongue-lashed by his wife for his carelessness. A dog took a notion to indulge in a swim, which so alarmed his master that he partially undressed, with the intention of swimming after the animal, when some one suggested that he first whistle. He adopted the suggestion and the dog responded to the call.

Mostly all the dwelling houses on the lower side of Second avenue at Soho are partially under water, and many families who in the morning had moved their household goods to the upper stories were in the afternoon taking them out of the upper windows. One poor woman, with a child in her arms, was crying piteously from the second story window of a frame house to take her out before the house and all was swept away. The water was then a considerable distance up the side of her dwelling.

A very amusing incident occurred yesterday afternoon on Seventh street, between Penn avenue and Duquesne way. Two men, standing to their waists in water, were fighting viciously for possession of a skiff. Finally one hit the other in the face and knocked him clean under water. At once overcome by a fear that the man might drown, the striker grabbed the strikee and pulled him to the surface. When the latter had spouted the water out of his mouth and cleared his eyes and ears, they compromised their differences, and getting into the skiff rowed away together.

* * * * * * *

TROUBLE AT THE THEATERS
No Performance Last Night
At Library Hall

No performance was given last night at Library Hall by Mr. Barrett and his company. The water had not only cut off street communications, but had flooded the first floor of the building and shut off the gas supply. Manger Parke authorizes the statement that all tickets sold for last night will be good for this evening, should he be able to give a performance, or for any other evening this week, or for Saturday's matinee.

The usual afternoon and evening entertainments were given at the Academy of Music. At Harris' Museum nothing was done owing to the depth of water on the pavement.

Everything considered, there was a fair audience last night at the Opera House, where the weakness in the supply of gaslight was made up by the addition of electric lights.

Oliver Doud Byron, who is underlined for next week at the Opera House, telegraphed yesterday to his manager to arrange for a matinee next Wednesday for the benefit of the sufferers.

THE CURIOUS CROWDS

As the water gradually increased upon the streets, it drove back, inch by inch, thousands of spectators, who filled every available space where the faintest glimpse might be caught of the turbulent tide. The streets in many parts of the city being navigable, small boats proved a source of constant attraction to the populace, and boats intended solely for the accommodation of those actually in need of them were monopolized almost exclusively by persons wishing to enjoy the once-in-a-life-time chance of a boat ride over the car tracks.

[The river?] drove away every animate object out of its course, created a silent panic among the beholders, and seemed to charm them where they stood, until brought to consciousness by finding themselves surrounded by the rising water.

* * * * * * *

SHELTER FOR THE HOMELESS

The reception room at City Hall was a curious spectacle last night. It was filled with men, women and children who had been driven out of their houses at the Point. All were furnished food from a neighboring restaurant at the Mayor's expense. There were at least a dozen families in the party, and none had saved any household goods. The children ranged from four months to twelve years of age. They enjoyed themselves at playing games in the Council chambers and using the roller chairs as velocipedes. The sufferers were furnished with blankets by the Mayor. A number of other families were quartered at the Froshinn, Lafayette and Moran's halls and in other parts of the city. The Mayor has notified all station house Captains to give the homeless shelter and food at his expense.

A PROCLAMATION
The Following Proclamation Has
Been Issued by Mayor Lyon:

Mayor's Office, Pittsburgh, Feb. 6, 1884 –

WHEREAS, The sudden rise in our rivers has caused great destruction of property and consequent distress to many of our citizens, I deem it my duty to take such action as will tend to alleviate the sufferings of those who are in actual need.

NOW, THEREFORE, I, Robert W. Lyon, Mayor of the city of Pittsburgh, do call upon our citizens generally, to assemble in the Select council chamber this (Thursday) afternoon at 3:30 o'clock, to take such action in the premises as may seem to them proper.

Robert W. Lyon, Mayor

A special meeting of both branches of Allegheny Councils has been called for nine o'clock this morning, to take some action in regard to relieving the sufferers by the flood.

* * * * * * *

DROWNED AT LIMERICK

Thomas Kelly, fifty-five years old, father of Boss Puddler Kelly, of the Clinton Rolling Mills, was drowned in the Monongahela last night. He started out in a boat to catch driftwood, and in trying to manage a heavy piece of timber just above the Point bridge his boat upset, and before assistance could be rendered he was drowned. A party of men secured his body and brought it to the shore.

* * * * * * *

DISABLED PRESSES

Most of the newspapers were discommoded as well as other people by the flooding of their press rooms. *The Post* this morning makes a draft for press work on the capacity of Williams' job rooms, Diamond street, and the *Commercial Gazette* relies on the courtesy of the *Leader* for the use of its press to enable it to get before the public. The *Times* press room is also flooded, and the *Dispatch*, too, suffers to some extent.

* * * * * * *

AS WE GO TO PRESS

At 2 o'clock this morning, shortly before *The Post* goes to press, there was 33 feet 9 inches of water in the Monongahela, and 34 feet 6 inches in the Allegheny, and both about stationary. It was raining hard."

* * * * * * *

". . . DRIFTWOOD

The insufficient supply of gas made the streets quite dark last night, and afforded thieves a fine opportunity to work.

An unusual number of people watched the flood record which is painted on a house at Penn and Water streets. The record back to '32 was beaten before 3 o'clock in the afternoon.

The coal men say their craft is safe.

The oldest inhabitant was outdone yesterday.

Had people given heed to the general warning issued from the headwaters of the Signal Service they would have been in better condition to receive the flood.

Several small shanty boats were sunk yesterday.

Several Pleasant Valley street cars are stranded on Ninth street.

The running of trains for the accommodation of those who live in Allegheny was commenced yesterday afternoon between the Union depot and the Federal street depot, Allegheny, and by their aid thousands were enabled to get home who would otherwise have only done so with great difficulty.

Yesterday afternoon as Miss Carrie Lyon, daughter of Mayor Lyon, and Miss Mary Lock and Miss Lizzie Michaels, of the south Side, were attempting to reach Curry Institute in a wagon, they fell out into the water. They suffered no serious injury beyond fright.

J. M. Gusky offers in another column to start with $500 a list of donations for the benefit of the sufferers.

A frame house belonging to Thomas Perry, on the River Road, Thirty-sixth ward, was lifted from its foundation by the water and placed on the bank with the front door horizontal to the ground.

A gang of laborers are kept busy clearing away rocks that roll down from Mt. Washington on the tracks of the Pan-handle railroad.

The Thirty-Sixth ward station house, South Side, is completely filled with water, and approach is cut off for more than a hundred feet surrounding it.

Deputy Mayor Lohrman, of the South Side, has rented the Phoenix Theatre and offers it as an abiding place for washed out families. It was well filled before midnight last night.

Fire alarm boxes Nos. 2, 15 and 21, along the wharf, are under water.

The sub-basement of the First National Bank building, Fifth avenue and Wood street, was flooded last night. The water is within an inch of the Receiving Department of the Western Union telegraph office.

The shoe store under Hugus & Hacke's store, Fifth avenue and Market street, and the one under Elsner & Phillips', Fifth avenue and Wood street, were flooded out.

City Hall was the most dismal looking place in the city last night. There was no gas in the building and the whole building was illuminated with a solitary candle.

Early this morning people were scouring the city for beds. All the hotels were filled. Those that were not flooded with water were overflowing with patrons.

* * * * * * *

UP THE ALLEGHENY
AT OIL CITY
Not So High as Last Year – Railroads
Greatly Inconvenienced

(Special to *The Pittsburgh Post*)

Oil City, February 6 – 10:30 P. M. – Rain commenced falling after midnight last night and continued until this afternoon. Since noon the water has fallen a foot. The railroads are greatly inconvenienced by water-covered tracks and land slides. The flood has not approached within five feet of last year's high water. It has commenced raining again this evening.

* * * * * * *

UP THE YOUGH
AT CONNELLSVILLE
The Biggest River in Ten Years – The
Waters Receding and No Further
Danger Feared

230

(Special to *The Pittsburgh Post*)

Connellsville, Pa., February 6 – Not for ten years has the Youghiogheny reached such a stage as it did at an early hour this morning, when the yellow foam-flecked waters swept by Water street, within two feet of its level. Cellars were flooded and some damage is reported. The water began to fall about six o'clock and has slowly receded ever since. Tonight it is six feet lower than it was this morning and all danger from the flood is believed to be at an end. The village of Yowlersville, submerged last Thursday when the ice went out, was again inundated, but the gradual rising of the waters enabled the inhabitants to retreat in good time and in good order, so that no loss of life or damage to household effects were sustained. The ferry house at Layton was swept away and several buildings at Jacob's creek joined in the downward journey. On the Baltimore and Ohio road, between here and Pittsburgh, numerous land slides have conspired all day to delay trains more or less, but the tracks are in good shape tonight, and no further trouble is anticipated. A big slide occurred at Broadford this forenoon, but a force of one hundred men were put to work at once, and trains succeeded in getting by this forenoon. The same trouble was experienced on the Fayette county branch, but the east end, from here to Cumberland, is all right, and no trouble is anticipated. The railroad was badly flooded, and trains were not running today. The Southwest, running across the country, experienced no trouble. The Baltimore and Ohio engine house at this place was struck by a land slide today, and the side next to the hill crushed in, necessitating the immediate removal of the locomotives.

A track walker on the B. & O. road, at Layton's, named Forsythe, was fatally injured this morning while engaged removing a slide from the road, and died this evening. He was working at the west bound track, when the express east, which was behind time, struck him, injuring him about the head and breaking one leg so badly that amputation was necessary. He leaves a wife and eight children.

* * * * * * *

MEADVILLE, PA
The People Traveling About the City in Boats

Meadville, Pa., February 6 – 10 P. M. – A special reports the western and southern parts of the city inundated. People go to and from their homes there in boats. All factories were compelled to shut down and the schools were mostly closed. Trains on the Meadville railway were abandoned. There are a few passenger trains running on the New York, Pittsburgh, and Ohio.

AID FOR THE SUFFERERS
Five Hundred Dollars Contributed by J. M. Gusky to Start a Flood Relief Fund

To *The Post* – The suffering and damage caused by the present extraordinary floods are of such a serious character that immediate steps are necessary to relieve the sufferers. I would therefore suggest donations be solicited from the business men of the two cities; and will myself start the list with a donation of $500 (five hundred dollars). I would further suggest that the Mayors of the two cities appoint committees to take charge and manage the funds contributed. Many of our business men, I think, will gladly contribute clothing, groceries, coal and other articles for the sufferers. The need is great, and prompt action necessary.

Respectfully yours,

J. M. Gusky

* * * * * * *

POSTSCRIPT
4:30 A.M.

FURTHER FLOOD NEWS
Deplorable State of Affairs in Allegheny
Rescue of the Residents of Brunot's Island
Additional Allegheny News
Further Details of the Inundation on the North Side

The following particulars of the flood in Allegheny City are in addition to the details in the first edition of *The Post:*

The Union bridge was rumored to be on its way South, and at dark it was still in position. It is evident that the piers have been weakened. Last evening a well-authenticated report stated that the first span on the Allegheny shore had been swept away. It was impossible to get within several squares of the bridge, and the darkness prevented the wreck, if such there was, being seen.

The transportation of families from their homes to dry land, and of workmen to their half submerged homes, at six o'clock last evening, caused all the streets in the flooded section to be crowded with skiffs, and beacon fires to be lighted at every corner where it was possible. The confusion that followed caused several accidents. On Isabella street a skiff containing a woman and three children was upset, but all were rescued by ready hands. Mrs. Donnelly attempted to drop into a skiff from a second story window of the Girard House on Federal street, which Officers Schuff [Scnuff?] and Munder had brought to her rescue, but missed her calculations and fell into the water. She was easily rescued. A young man on a raft while paddling around Madison avenue, was caught by the current, and was being swept out into midstream, when he was noticed by four young men in a skiff. On their approach the man thoughtlessly jumped into the skiff and overturned it. A man named McKelvey happened to be near with another skiff, and rescued the five who were in the water with great difficulty.

About five o'clock a house at the corner of Sandusky streets was discovered to be on fire. A still alarm was sent to the Columbia engine house, and that company responded in skiffs. A portion of the roof was burned.

Of the many families who moved from their houses, a large number were unable to find shelter. City Hall was thrown open to them, and last evening the offices of the Poor Board, Water Assessor, Superintendent of the Water Works, two committee rooms and the two Council chambers, were either occupied or ready to be occupied. About twenty families were sheltered there, and others under directions of the Mayor were being brought there at every hour during the night. The Mayor provided each with supper at the city's expense. Today there will probably be a large number of people there, and all who can are requested to lend assistance toward providing for them.

At the Riverside Penitentiary the prison yard is completely submerged. The water is in the cellar, but the coverings over all the openings allowed only a small quantity to enter. Three steam siphons kept the water in the cellar low enough to permit the operation of the heating apparatus.

Oliver's mill and that large section of low lying ground west of Preble avenue extension is covered to a depth of ten or twelve feet. All along the river in the Ninth and Sixth wards the water is over the bank, and extends from one to two squares inland. From Page street southward Beaver avenue is impassable, and the two squares between that and the river are completely submerged. Rebecca street, from end to end, is covered to a depth of seven to eight feet. All the mills, the steel works and gas works were under water almost to the roof. The dwellings on River avenue are under water to their second stories. High board fences have entirely disappeared. Houses on the upper side of Rebecca street are flooded to the depth of six and eight feet. At School street the water pushes out its limit again till it is stopped by the steep cliffs of Monument Hill. The P., Ft. W. & C. R. R. embankment from Marion avenue to Federal street limits the breadth of the river there. For six squares deep, and from School street to Federal street the water rises to the height of the second and third stories, and some of the smaller houses are completely submerged. On Federal street the water line lies between the railroad and Lacock street. East of that the West Penn railroad embankment checks the water's spread. Between Sandusky and Anderson streets the water is six feet deep at the embankment. Along that portion of the road neighboring houses have been connected with the road by plank bridges thrown from the second-story window. The water touches the ceilings of the first floor of these houses. People may be seen lifting the water for cooking purposes into their second-story windows by means of buckets at the end of a line, and in that portion can the misery arising from the crowded condition of the houses and the high water be most plainly seen. The large furniture factory is covered almost to the second floor. At the Railroad bridge just the top of a lamp post indicates where the street is, and the depth of the flood. From there eastward the same picture of half submerged houses, streets crowded with boats, and down between the houses can be seen a narrow strip of the river sweeping its burden of ice onward.

Kopp & Voegtley's large saw mill is almost entirely covered, and has been lifted considerably out of its position. The Globe and Eagle varnish works are indicated by the tops of their smoke stacks, by floating tanks and a heavy coating of oil on the water. The Globe Company fixes their loss in stock alone at $10,000. The loss to the Eagle Company is not so great.

At the Water Works a strange sight was to be seen. The water covered the floor of the engine room to the depth of six inches. As the huge crank and fly wheel slowly revolved hundreds of gallons of water were thrown out of the fly wheel pit as the crank in the wheel came up. The pumps were buried under twenty feet of water, and the only indication of the heavy machinery at work down below was the surging and boiling of the water at the surface of the pit. In the boiler room the water was within three inches of the grate bars at ten o'clock last night. The firemen had heaped up the fuel to a height of eight feet, and there, perched on top of the heap, surrounded by six feet of water, they supplied the furnaces.

At Groetzinger's large new tannery the water flooded the building to the second floor. It reached the lime house, which adjoins the bark house, and before anyone was aware the bark was on fire. It was extinguished with great difficulty, but without calling out the department.

The new Herr's Island bridge, but recently erected by the city at a cost of over $16,000, was the center of great attraction. The river at four o'clock was level with the floor. The ice and drift filled the narrow channel from shore to shore, and was running with tremendous force. For three hours, to the surprise of all, it stood the terrible trial. A heavy barge bearing a derrick crashed against it with all the force of the current, and a huge ice gorge, but it did not yield. The barge lodged there and materially narrowed the channel. Just as preparations were being made to blow the barge up with dynamite the north end of the bridge broke from the heavy anchorage, swung down the stream and a moment later the bridge sunk from sight.

236

Shortly before it gave way a rabbit was seen riding down the turbid stream on a cake of ice. As it neared the churning crashing maelstrom bunny saw his danger. With all his power he sprang from cake to cake, from log to log. The crowd watched the little gray beauty striving for his life. Though every muscle was strained to its utmost he gained not an inch. Exhausted, he paused for a moment, and in that moment was swept into the hell that raged around him. A loud cheer broke from the crowed the next second, for there, with ears erect, and gracefully poised on a cake of ice bunny went sailing on down the river.

Last night was a night of darkness. Not a cubic foot of gas was burned in the city except at the Western Penitentiary. That building is supplied by its own works. Federal and Ohio streets, Beaver avenue and Spring Garden avenue were in almost utter darkness. A few dismal rays from an oil lamp in a store window here and there made the darkness the more intense. People on the streets carried lamps. The appearance of the city was so unusual that one could not but feel that some great calamity had befallen it. The quiet back streets and alleys were places to be avoided, as it was just as easy to walk through an unknown coal mine without lamp or torch as tread the streets of Allegheny.

The engine houses and City Hall were made less dark by a few tallow candles and gasoline lamps. This crowd of miserable and bedraggled people gather at City Hall for shelter, gave that place an air of unutterable sadness, which seemed to extend thence over the whole of the dark and flooded city.

Late last evening a report reached the city that the people of Brunot's Island had been driven from their homes by the flood. They have not been as fortunate as the people of Herr's Island in escaping to the main land. The report said that the men, women and children had taken refuge in the trees, and that their screams for help could be heard all over Woods Run. Two boats lying at the wharf there could not reach the Island on account of the current, and the people were perishing from cold and exhaustion. It was found that of the five families living on the island all were in a desperate strait. The island was completely covered, and all the inhabitants were driven to the upper stories and roofs of their houses. The steamboats *James Brown* and *Phoenix*, after a long struggle, rescued the people by going over to the island from the back river[1].

It was reported at an early hour this morning that the Little Junction and Herr's Island bridges have been washed away by the flood. The Sharpsburg bridge is several feet under water.

THE WATER AT 3:30

At 3:30 this morning the stage of water in the Monongahela was still 33 feet 9 inches and standing. A drizzling rain had been falling since midnight. The few river men who were loitering about at that time insist that the end is not yet. They predict higher water for today.

* * * * * * *

THEY STILL REMEMBER IT

The residents of Spring Garden avenue, Allegheny, were greatly alarmed last night. They were fearful of the sewers backing up and causing a repetition of the disastrous flood of 1874.

* * * * * * *

---

[1]There is no record of these two steamboats in Capt. Fred Way's *Packet Directory* or the *Lytle-Holdcamper List*. See bibliography.

HEAVY SALE OF TICKETS

Over 4,000 tickets were sold at the Allegheny depot for the 15-minute train on the Ft. Wayne [rail]road between Pittsburgh and Allegheny."

⁐

— 44 —

Pittsburgh Morning Post, April 7, 1886
"RIVER RAVAGES

Great Damage Caused by Flood and Rain —
Families in the Low Lands Desert Their Homes.
Landslides Interrupt Passenger and Freight Traffic.
Mills and Workshops Closed Down by the High Water.

* * * * * * *

The situation along the river fronts last night was grave and somewhat alarming. At midnight both streams were swelling at the rate of two inches an hour, and the marks showed twenty-two feet seven inches in the Monongahela and twenty-three feet one inch in the Allegheny. Late advices from the headwaters reported both streams rising at all points, and seemed to bear out the predictions of old and experienced river men of a dangerous and disastrous stage of water. Much damage and inconvenience have been already caused by the heavy rains and high waters, and more will doubtless be experienced before the rivers recede. Signal Service estimates place the maximum proportions of the present flood at some few feet below that of 1884, and indicate that the waters will have done their worst by noon of today.

* * * * * * *

THROUGHOUT THE TWO CITIES
Effects of the Rains and High Waters
in All Quarters.

At 9 o'clock yesterday morning the stage of water in the Monongahela was sixteen feet full, having risen two feet since 9 o'clock the previous night. At 10 o'clock the marks read seventeen feet, at 11 o,clock eighteen feet was recorded and at noon nineteen feet six inches was the stage. At 2:30 o'clock in the afternoon the marks showed twenty-one feet and the river was rising slowly. At 6 o'clock there was but twenty-one feet four inches and at 11 o'clock last night the stage was twenty-two feet scant. Up to noon the damage along the Monongahela had been comparatively slight, as precautions had been taken against losses by unusually high water. The Point population had made preparations to move, and manufacturers and business men had cleared out their cellars of perishable articles and removed them to upper stories. On the South side, from Thirtieth to Thirty-sixth streets, everything was on the move. Cellars were filling up rapidly. At Oliver Bros. & Phillips, Fifteenth Street Mill preparations were being made to close down, and twenty-three feet would close Oliver's Tenth Street Mill, as the water backs up in the fly-wheel pit. It was thought by the lower South Side mill men that by night almost every mill along the Monongahela river would be closed up. In the Thirty-fifth ward, the bridge over Sawmill Run was carried away with a big crash about 2 o'clock yesterday morning. The water in the run was very high, and a panic seemed to strike the residents thereabouts. Dozens of them made their appearance in scanty attire and debated excitedly the prospects of being swept away. The West End gas works was submerged yesterday morning for over an hour, and street Commissioner Fording had to do some active work to get the water out.

THE ALLEGHENY

Commenced to rise early yesterday morning, and so suddenly and rapidly did the water creep up the bank that when daylight broke, Sandy Creek, above Sharpsburg, was mostly under water, and the waves were at the doors and in some cases dangerously near second-story windows. The place is the home of many mill hands and miners, and they were compelled to go to their work in boats, moving their families to places of safety, however, before they went. Several houses looked as if ready to set sail, and the probabilities were a considerable amount of damage would be done before the water receded. All the low-lying lands from Sharpsburg down were inundated, in some places to a depth of several feet. Lawrencevillians were extremely nervous, and residents along the river were moving their valuable household articles to neighboring houses high up the hill. Nearly all the mills were either shut down or preparing to do so, as at 6 o'clock the indications were that every mill within a hundred yards of the bank would be compelled to stop operations. Precautions were being taken in all directions, and the Fire Department was holding itself in readiness to assist in saving property if the flood should reach anything like the proportions of the one of 1884. At 12 o'clock the stream had swollen to a height of twenty-two feet, and was rising so slowly that hopes were entertained it would not exceed twenty-six or twenty-seven feet. The damage up to that hour was comparatively trifling and a very much easier feeling prevailed.

ON THE NORTH SIDE

The heavy rains of Monday night did a considerable amount of damage in Allegheny. The water poured down Troy and Spring Hills in torrents and many residents in that vicinity were for a while disposed to fly for safety and leave their household effects to the mercy of the elements. They were principally alarmed by the danger that threatened their homes by the washing away of the foundation. Landslides were started by the constant rains, and they came down like avalanches against the dwellings in their path and on to the thoroughfares until some of them were simply impassable. About four hundred feet of the crest of the hill near the Spring Garden avenue car stables became detached and came thundering down on to Wickline Lane, so effectually blockading it that it was necessary to clear away some of the dirt before travel along that thoroughfare could be resumed.

A large retaining wall on the property of Mr. Buchr[?], a saloonkeeper, was so damaged that it gave way and fell. The wall was twelve feet high and forty feet in length. A large mass of earth was carried down Spring Hill and lodged on Humboldt street.

The occupants of the houses in Smith's row, on Gallagher street, Second ward, were compelled to move their household goods to the third floor. The houses are close the back of the hill, and the water which came down over it found its way in at the second story.

The properties of Mr. John Miller and Mrs. Nichols were so damaged by the waters that poured down from a Bluff street quarry, that they stated they would institute suits against the city for damages.

All along the north shore of the Allegheny yesterday was presented a scene of great animation. Those who had property in imminent danger were taking active measures to secure it. All sorts of craft moored along the bank received additional ropes and chains, while lumber and kindred property disappeared as if by magic from the water's edge. The residents of the Fourth ward, along River avenue, were thoroughly aroused, and were preparing for another 1884 experience. Cellars were filled with water and the people were holding themselves in readiness to move up close to the roof.

DETENTION TO TRAINS
The Allegheny Valley Railroad Entirely Stopped.

Nearly every train that came into the Union Depot last evening was behind time, as a result of the storm of the past two days. Travel was also very light, it seeming that persons had concluded to stay at home rather than run the risk of delays incident to the weather. The most serious trouble occurred upon the Allegheny Valley road. Trains were delayed from four to six hours on this road, on account of land slides, and in the afternoon the management decided to stop the sale of tickets over that road altogether, until the weather improves and the road is placed in a safe condition. Persons who were in the city and desirous of getting home over that road, were therefore compelled to remain here and make the best of the circumstances. One train got in yesterday afternoon, but it took from 8 o'clock in the morning until 2 o'clock in the afternoon to run from Kittanning to the city, a frequent stops were necessary to shovel dirt rocks from the tracks."

Bibliography

Baldwin, Leland D. *The Keelboat Age On Western Waters.* Pittsburgh: University of Pittsburgh Press, 1941.

_____. *Pittsburgh: The Story of a City.* Pittsburgh: University of Pittsburgh Press, 1937. Paper reprint, 1970.

Brownsville American Telegraph, 1816.

Caldwell, J.A. *Caldwell's Illustrated Combination Centennial Atlas of Washington Co. Pennsylvania. 1876.* Rimerstown, Pa.: Pennsylvania Record Press, 1976. Reprint by the Ft. Vance Historical Society, Burgettstown, Pa.

Corddry, Gannett Fleming and Carpenter, Inc. *A History of Navigation Improvements on the Monongahela River.* Pittsburgh: For the U.S. Army Corps of Engineers, Pittsburgh District, March, 1980.

Cramer, Zadok. *The Navigator; containing directions for navigation The Monongahela, Allegheny, Ohio and Mississippi Rivers; With an ample account of these much Admired waters, from the head of the former to the mouth of the latter; and a concise description of these towns, villages, harbors, settlements, &c. with maps of the Ohio and Mississippi.* Pittsburgh: John Scull, et al, 1802, 1806, 1808.

Ellis, Franklin, ed. *History of Fayette County, Pennsylvania, with Biographical Sketches of Many of its Pioneers and Prominent Men.* Philadelphia: L.H. Everts & Co., 1882. Reprint, 1986.

Folmar, John Kent, and William F. Trimble. *Forging A Society: Readings in the History of Western Pennsylvania, 1748-1877.* Pittsburgh: The Historical Society of Western Pennsylvania, 1982. Published by J.K. Folmar, 1983.

Folmar I, J.K. *Drifting Back in Time: Historical Sketches of Washington and Fayette Counties, Pennsylvania, including the Monongahela River Valley.* California, Pa.: Yohogania Press, 2005.

Gannett Fleming Corddry and Carpenter. *A History of Navigation Improvements on the Monongahela River.* Pittsburgh: U.S. Corps of Engineers, Pittsburgh District, March, 1980.

Gates, John K. *In Other Years; Uniontown and Southern Fayette County.* Uniontown:Photographit, 1979.

Harris' Intelligencer (Pittsburgh), 1839.

History of Allegheny Co., Pennsylvania, With Illustrations Descriptive Residences, Public Buildings, Fine Blocks, and Important Manufactories, from original Sketches by artists of the highest ability. Philadelphia: L.H. Everts & Co., 1876.

Hunter, Louis C. *Steamboats on the Western Rivers: An Economic and Technological History.* New York: Dover Publications, 1977.

Johnson, Dr. Leland R. *The Headwaters District: A History of the Pittsburgh District, U.S. Army Corps of Engineers.* Pittsburgh: U.S. Army Corps of Engineers, Pittsburgh District, n.d.

Jones, S., *Pittsburgh in the Year Eighteen Hundred and Twenty-six, containing Sketches Topographical, Historical and Statistical; together with A Directory of the City, and A View of its Various Manufactures, Population, Improvements, &c.* Pittsburgh: Johnston & Stockton, 1826.

Kelly, George E., ed. *Allegheny County: A Sesqui-Centennial Review, 1788-1938.* Pittsburgh: Allegheny County Susqui-Centennial Committee, 1938.

Killikelly, Sarah H. *The History of Pittsburgh Its Rise and Progress.* Pittsburgh: B.C. & Gordon Montgomery Co., 1906.

Klein, Philip S. and Ari Hoogenboom. *A History of Pennsylvania.* New York: McGraw- Hill Book Co., 1973.

Lorant, Stephen, et al. *Pittsburgh: The Story of An American City.* Lenox, Mass.: Updated and enlarged ed., R.R. Donnelley & Sons Co., 1975.

Lytle, William M., and Forrest R. Holdcamper, Rev & ed, C. Bradford Mitchell with Kenneth R. Hall. *Merchant Steam Vessels of the United States, 1790-1868.* Steamship Historical Society of America, 1952. Reprint, 1975, ditto; dist. by The University of Baltimore Press, Baltimore.

McCullough, Robert and Walter Leuba, *The Pennsylvania Main Line Canal. York, Pa.:* The American Canal and Transportation Center, 1973. Reprint, 1976.

McFarland, Joseph F. *20th Century History of the City of Washington and Washington County Pennsylvania and Representative Citizens.* Chicago: Richmond-Arnold Publishing Co., 1910.

Monongahela Daily Republican, 1840, 1880.

Pittsburgh Gazette, 1786-1837.

Pittsburgh Daily Gazette, 1849-1873.

Pittsburgh (Morning/Daily) Post, 1858-1886.

Reiser, Catherine Elizabeth. *Pittsburgh's Commercial Development, 1800-1850*. Harrisburg: Pennsylvania Historical and Museum Commission, 1951.

Rice, Otis K. *West Virginia: A History.* Lexington, Ky.: The University of Kentucky Press, 1985.

Stover, John F. *History of the Baltimore and Ohio Railroad.* W. Lafayette, Ind.: Purdue University Press, 1987. Paper reprint, 1995.

Tenth Annual Report, of the President and Managers, to the Monongahela Navigation Company; Presented January, l850, with the Accompanying Documents. Pittsburgh: Johnson and Stockton, 1850.

U.S., *Allegheny & Monongahela Rivers Navigation Charts.* Pittsburgh: U.S. Army Corps of Engineers District, Jan., 1973.

U.S., *Ohio River Navigation Charts.* Pittsburgh: U.S. Army Corps of Engineers Pittsburgh District, Jan., 1985.

Way, Frederick, Jr., comp;, *Way's Packet Directory, 1848-1983, Passenger Steamboats of the Mississippi River System Since the Advent of Photography in Mid-Continent America.*. Athens, O.: Ohio University, 1983.

_____, With Joseph W. Rutter. *Way's Steam Towboat Directory.* Athens, O.: Ohio University Press, 1990.

Wiley, Richard T. *Elizabeth and Her Neighbors.* Richard T. Wiley: 1936. Reprint, Clossen Press, 1997.

Wallace, Paul A.W., revised, William A. Hunter, *Indians in Pennsylvania,* Anthropological Series, No. 5. Harrisburg: The Pennsylvania Historical and Museum Commission, 1989.

Workers of the Writers' Program of the Works Progress Administration in the Commonwealth of Pennsylvania. *The Story of Old Allegheny City.* Pittsburgh: Allegheny Centennial Committee, 1941.

Index